Crazy
Creek

SARAH SIMPSON BIVENS

ISBN: 10: 1511525088
ISBN-13: 978-1511525084

DEDICATION

To the memory of my parents,
Ben B. and Annie Laura Harrison Simpson,
who shared their love of the written word,
to Maggie C. LeNoir,
an English teacher at Loudon High School, who
was the first to encourage me
to become a writer,
and to Dan Hicks, Jr., who was the first to hire me
as a feature writer,
I dedicate this novel as a tribute
of my appreciation.
People pass away but their influence lives on.

PREFACE

Although the story, events and characters are completely fictitious, much of the information given as background information is true, notably actions taken by the Tennessee Valley Authority which, to date, has built 29 hydro-electric dams, many located in East Tennessee.

Also, historical reference to the development of the Tennessee Walking Horse stated the name of a real horse and its owner as well as factual issues pertaining to the breed.

ACKNOWLEDGMENTS

I am extremely grateful to numerous people for contributions to the writing of this novel: my friend and former bookstore owner, Brenda Lambert, for her positive comments about the manuscript, my old friends James and Susan Moser for the many trail rides we shared with James as the guide into the mountains and back country around Citico and beyond, Dr. Bob Womack for his research and book *Echoes of Hoofbeats,* and the Brantley family from Middle Tennessee for their contribution to my knowledge and love of the Tennessee Walking Horse. Lastly, I wish to thank my husband Ron Bivens for his much appreciated patience while I struggled with the computer.

PROLOGUE
Background: 1933 -1972

Emmett Moss could not remember a time when he didn't have a keen distrust of government. And he had good reason for the way he felt. He was little more than a toddler back in the '40's when his family was forcibly removed from their fertile and productive farm located high on a mountain along the border between North Carolina and Tennessee. Although he was too young at the time to understand the turmoil surrounding their move, he nonetheless saw and felt the sadness and anger around him. Throughout the years that followed, he had heard the story told and retold. There was no question in his mind, then nor now, that government was the enemy.

Before the move, Emmett's father made a good living raising produce, mainly green beans, tomatoes, and corn, and selling it to the local cannery. The cannery not only paid the farmers, they also provided jobs with reasonable wages to many in the area. Life was good, with only the weather and black bears, and of course, the war, to worry about. But the powerful government entity, The Tennessee

Valley Authority, known mostly by its initials, TVA, decided to take their land for another one of their dams. Douglas Dam in Sevier County, Tennessee, was going to be built about the same time as the Fontana Dam. In fact, the two dams would be built in adjoining counties, but separated by the state line. Douglas would back up waters of the French Broad River which absorbs the Pigeon River, the Nolichucky and Holston Rivers and comes together to form the Tennessee River in Knoxville. Fontana would impound a large area of North Carolina.

Created by Congressional Charter back in 1933, TVA promised it would bring economic development and flood control to the region by producing more electricity. That was given as reason enough to take land from the people who owned it. A U.S. Senator from Oklahoma by the name of Norris was the chief promoter of TVA. It seemed strange to the people who lived in East Tennessee that someone from way off in Oklahoma wanted to create an agency that was supposed to help them. Why not build dams there, they asked. No one ever answered their questions. The lobbyists and bureaucrats pushed hard; thus, TVA was created and the big new government agency repaid the Oklahoma senator by naming its first hydroelectric dam after him. Norris Dam was built in 1936 in East Tennessee.

After Japan dropped bombs on Pearl Harbor in '41, TVA no longer needed a hard sell to build more dams because they could use the war as justification. Everyone wanted to win the war. Since metal was needed for equipment and metal manufacturing needed electricity, just about everyone was convinced that more hydroelectric dams were needed. The only people who stood in the way were the poor, beleaguered citizens in East Tennessee and North Carolina who would have to be removed from the lands and homes they owned. Now that TVA used the war as their primary justification for building more dams, the public didn't seem to mind the injustice done to the mountain people who would have to give up, under the law of Eminent Domain, what they had rightfully attained.

Emmett's family was one of the 525 families literally pushed out of their homes and off their farms to make way for the Douglas Dam. They were paid little for the 33,160 acres which had been fought and died for by their ancestors back in the Revolutionary War. It was their Scotch-Irish ancestors who had climbed the harsh terrain and discovered the lush flat and fertile plain high above the cities and towns below them. There was no way the little money paid them could purchase anything as good as what they had. The Douglas Dam flooded 40 square miles of fertile land and wiped out the cannery and 32 cemeteries.   In North Carolina's Swain and Graham counties which bordered Sevier and Blount counties in Tennessee, the Fontana Dam took 68,292 acres and removed 1,311 families and 1,047 graves. The town of Fontana had been thriving mainly from lumber and copper mining operations high up on Yellow Creek Mountain. In addition to the losses suffered by land owners, the Fontana impoundment inundated the towns of Bushnell, Forney and Judson, as well as Fontana. The only thing that remained of that town was its name. In addition to the acreage that TVA took, 40,000 more acres were deeded over to the Great Smoky National Park and even more to the national forests. It was almost as if the government was determined to wipe out the entire mountain population and its culture. These two dams were begun in '42; Douglas was completed in '43 and Fontana in '44.

Emmett's family, along with some of the other ousted families relocated in the mountains near a place called Jensen's Valley. His father could no longer make a living selling produce as he had before. In the first place, the only land he could afford to buy did not lay well and was not suitable for major cultivation. In the second place, there was no cannery to sell to. He was hard pressed to know how he was going to provide for his family. They would have to live mostly off the land, but there was one thing he knew how to do, and now he had no reservation about doing it. That was making and selling liquor. Emmett's father knew it was illegal to sell moonshine and before, in his old life, he had made it rarely and for his own personal use, to share with friends around a campfire while they listened to the hounds run fox. Now that the government had become the enemy, he had lost all respect for the law. Yes, he decided, he would break the government's law. He would make whiskey and sell it.

Now, here it was 1972. Little Emmett had grown up and taken up his father's trade, having learned it as a boy. It was a good thing because his father had died suddenly under the limb of an old oak tree which fell on him as he was walking from the garden to his house. Suddenly, Emmett had to help provide for his mother and younger brothers and sisters. Although this new mountain community of Crazy Creek had become home, he could still remember the look in his parents eyes as they looked into their past. They knew the jokes made about mountaineers, knew they were referred to as ridgerunners, they heard the comments made about their manner of speech which some linguists referred to as Smoky Mountain talk and others called old world dialect handed down from their Scotch and Irish ancestors. They continued to be a proud and independent people with a deep distrust of government and some town people who didn't have a clue about real mountain life.

About the only government worker Emmett trusted at all was young Tish Jamison. He trusted her not because of her current position as a social worker with a state agency but because of what she did when she was a child. He remembered how she would stand up to the big older kids in defense of his little nephew Davy who was bullied badly during those years when they attended school in Jensen's Valley. Emmett was in the eighth grade when he watched Tish defend Davy. It was during that year his father had died and he had to drop out of school. Emmett, however, continued to appreciate Tish now as he had way back then.

Emmett knew that many people favored TVA for providing good-paying jobs in the area. He wasn't sure how people were chosen for those jobs. They did hire some of the mountain people. Most of them took the jobs and were pragmatic about the situation. They knew if they didn't, someone else would. So, they took them and made more money than they had ever made in their lives. Yet, some of the mountain people, like Emmett, stuck by their principles and refused to work for an outfit that took people's land. It was just another reason for the mountain people to distrust outsiders and feel strong loyalty toward each other. As for electricity, they didn't miss what they had never had. They kept their food cold in the mountain streams. There was plenty of wood for fires they built in their big old pot-bellied stoves which would heat a cabin even if it had a few cracks showing between some of the logs. Fireplaces were a little different, sending most of the heat straight up the chimney, but they were good to sit around in winter, talking or playing music or just watching the flames dance among the logs.

CHAPTER ONE

Dust rolled in the windows of the old bus as it lurched over the bumpy Meadow Road. Flecks of it swirled in the air and finally settled on shiny foreheads as the odor of sweat started to permeate the air. Neither sweat nor dust were strangers to any of the passengers who lived mostly off the land. They were the rural poor, people who had settled the knobby hills which stepped from the fertile valley to the mountains. When prosperity had come to some in the picturesque valley, these people were left out. Through the government's condemnation of their land to make way for TVA dams and the Great Smoky Mountain National Park, they had been pushed to the backside of the region and were scattered all the way from the Smokies to the Nantahala range. There they enjoyed the back drop of another government acquisition, the Cherokee National

Forest. Unlike the families who had relocated in cities and towns in East Tennessee, North Georgia, and the northwestern portion of North Carolina, they would not leave their beloved mountains and clung to whatever spot of land they could find. One spot in particular caught their eye. It was where two creeks flowing down the mountain converged and seemed to fight each other as they sought to find a path to continue downward. The waters churned and bubbled in such a way that folks began to describe it as that old crazy creek. As families settled near it, the area took its name from the busy rushing whitewater.

Tish Jamison was not from one of the dislocated families, but having grown up in Jensen's Valley, the nearest town to Crazy Creek, she felt at home with them. She sat on the bus wondering if it was the same one she used to take to school; it was certainly old enough. As she gazed from the window at the creek flowing lazily now beside them, it's bends and twists matching those of the road, her mind wandered back nearly 20 years when she was a school girl traveling this same route. It was raining that day, the one she could see clearly in her mind's eye. She watched the memory unfold:

Joe Miller cursed as mud splattered the windshield. He stopped the bus by the mail box in front of the Moss place. Three little boys climbed aboard dripping water in the aisle. Their feet were bare, mud oozed from between their toes. A group of older boys sitting in the back of the bus began laughing and hissing.

Tish turned and shook her small fist at the jeering boys. Watching the tears that welled in the eyes of Davy Moss, crimson glowed from her own cheeks.

"Do you want to get a switching?" her sister Susan pinched her.

Tish was angry. It was terrible having two older sisters, Tish thought, especially when they were teenagers. They were too old to be any fun, but not old enough to be kind. Someday, she decided, turning her thoughts towards the rear of the bus, she would show those jackasses!

The bus lurched suddenly, making it possible for a deer to scurry across the road, interrupting Tish's memories and bringing her attention to the present. She studied the faces of those seated around her. Her old classmate, Davy, was not among them, but his uncle and cousins were.

Alex Morgan sat in his office wondering what Tish was doing at this very moment. He hated surprises but knew he was going to get one. She had promised him one. Although he claimed to have hired her to the Department of Human Services, he in fact had not. It was the State Personnel Office who had really hired her and sent her to the office which he supervised. She was to work with both children and adults in a pilot program designed especially for the region. He had no choice but to make the best of the situation because he sure did want to keep his job of having other people do most of the work. He figured the best way to get along was to avoid making waves. He put his feet on his desk and thought about leaving but realized it was early in the day and he had to be at the church for the opening program of the summer festival's music contest. Since it was a fundraiser for the needy, he definitely had to make a showing. Still, he resented having to go. It was Saturday and normally the office would be closed, but because of the event, it was going to be a work day. Besides, it was so hot, he might as well relax in his air-conditioned office and play solitaire until time to go. Pulling the deck of well-worn cards from the top drawer of his desk, he looked at his watch and wondered again what time Tish would return or even if she would. Chuckling to himself, he recalled how she had called him a jackass years ago when she was just a little tyke. During the two years she had worked with him, he heard the word often, but he was so pompous and sure of himself, he never suspected how often the word was used in reference to him.

Other members of the staff often looked at Tish in quiet admiration enjoying the outbursts which lightened the otherwise dreary meetings which Alex insisted upon. Among other things, he was boring.

Since Alex was safely out of the way in his office, Mabel, the receptionist, seized the opportunity to tell Jenny, a social worker who had just returned from vacation, about a recent staff meeting.

"Jenny, you missed a good one. Mr. Morgan read a letter from the State telling him to integrate the diverse socio-economic groups in the area by arranging joint cultural, social and/or religious meetings. After he finished the letter, everybody started offering suggestions about what we could do but Mr. Morgan just ignored everyone and looked at Tish. She said, 'Don't look at me, I have no sugges-tions,'" Mabel cleared her throat.

"What happened then?" Jenny asked.

"Tish looked him straight in the eye with that deadpan expression she can get and said real pro-fessional like that it would be a good idea to have some of the mountain folks serve moonshine to the town people. She said they'd all get happy then!"

Jenny smiled, "Oh, I wish I'd been there. I'll bet everyone had a good laugh."

"Yes, everyone but old Alex . . . excuse me, I meant to say Mister Morgan . . . he just ignored her comment and told her he was making it her respon-sibility to come up with something by the end of this week. So, we're all waiting to see what she does."

"Mabel, I don't care what you call him," Jenny gestured with her head to the Supervisor's office, "but I understand you want to show respect by ad-dressing him as 'Mister' in front of the public." Jenny said, smiling as she walked away to her cubi-cle.

Marlo Scott woke early Saturday morning. Her blonde curls, glistening from a hot shower, lent a girlish air to the young woman as she emptied a tray of ice cubes. She wondered if anyone else in Jensen's Valley had a Bloody Mary before going to church. But it wasn't really church, just a program being held in the church, she reasoned. She sipped hers thoughtfully. The glass was cold and felt good resting in her hand. It seemed to be the only thing that helped her relax anymore. She wondered again, as she did every day lately, if she were becoming an alcoholic. Maybe she was one already. Or, maybe she just liked it too much. She watched her trembling hands relax as she drained the glass. Dressing in a white linen sheath and soft kid shoes, she rationalized that it was necessary for someone playing the organ to play with steady hands. She wasn't sure why she had agreed to play; she just couldn't think of a reason not to. The chairman of the program committee thought perhaps there would be important guests attending and they would prefer to have someone highly trained like herself to play during the opening service at the church.

Marlo had no idea that she was the valley's most prestigious person. She was the beautiful daughter of one of the state's wealthiest families, appreciated because she chose to remain living there when her parents did not. The local merchants loved to see her shopping in their stores. They admired the grace of her finishing school charm and impeccable manners. It was Marlo who unknowingly set the fashion. When she favored a new style, the ladies of the town were quick to follow. She had in fact been elevated to almost a celebrity status. And, as a result, she was quite alone. Few invited her to their social gatherings thinking she would find them beneath her social standing. And though many young men admired her from afar, few were presumptuous enough to approach her.

Marlo could not understand why she was lonely, only that she was. Her natural reserve prevented her from initiating friendships. In earlier years, when she had dated boys, her shyness had been mistaken for lack of interest. Now, in her late twenties, the only people she felt comfortable with other than her family were the servants and her very special friends, Tish and Julie. The three of them had been inseparable when they were children. Only she had been sent away to an exclusive summer camp for part of each summer while they remained in the valley. When she was gone, she missed them terribly, wondering what fun things they were doing. As an only child, she thought of them as the sisters she didn't have. Now, though, they were always busy with their jobs and her parents preferred to spend most of their time in Florida. Marlo preferred the mountains and the valley, yet she spent many of her hours seated at the piano playing classical music or reading romantic novels and attending her private bar, alone.

Today was going to be different, she was at least going to get out of the house and do something. Marlo got into her sporty Mustang and headed away from the secluded estate onto Meadow Road. She lowered the window to enjoy the mountain breeze, but no sooner than she had, she rolled it back up again as Mr. Miller's old bus went by showering her with dust. She heard strains of the hymn "It's a Great Getting Up Morning" echoing from the bus and wondered where the people were going. Probably to another settlement, she thought, for a group baptism. Perhaps the shock of the cold, clear mountain stream would wash away some of her pain and disappointment. Maybe it would do more good than the tepid drop of water on her head had done when she was sprinkled in the Methodist church so many years ago. She longed for a renewed feeling of faith, somehow lost.

As the bus was nearing its destination in town, Tish felt a tug on her sleeve.

"Miss Tish, are you sure this is the right thing to do?" Emmett was leaning over the seat, his battered old straw hat crumpled in his hand.

"I'm not real sure if it's the right thing or not, but it should be fun anyway, don't you think? Just go along for the heck of it and see what comes of it."

"Go to church just for the hell of it!" Emmett had almost shouted.

His six children and Mattie, his wife, glared at Tish . Mattie said, "Lord, Miss Tish, you ought to be ashamed."

"You misunderstood . . . I didn't say 'hell', I said 'heck'."

"Same difference, ain't it?" Mattie asked, scowling at Tish.

"Well, I didn't mean it that way." Tish explained. "As I told you, this is not going to be a regular church service; it's an event that's going to be held in the church. It's kind of like having prayer before the contest begins. After this, we'll have our picnic and then go across the street to the Memorial Building where you all will play and sing, like we planned. The opening meeting, that's being held in the church, will give the townspeople a chance to get to know you better. The whole thing is a new activity organized to raise money for the needy."

"Miss Tish," Emmett said, "they know me as well as an old cat knows a hound, and that's plenty of knowin'. That bunch in that high-toned town church come out to Crazy Creek once a year bringing Christmas baskets like they're carrying tickets to the pearly gates. Do you remember when the Dobbs missus was dying? She lay up there helpless, sometimes screaming with pain, for nearly three months. Did they lift a finger to help then? Hell, no. But after she died, some of them fine ladies came up there and prayed over her, like none of us knowed how to pray. They turned up their noses at the Dobbs younguns' talkin' about how dirty they were. Well, what did they expect with their mother laid up so long? I heard one of them say that it'd be wasteful to give the kids anything because they were filthy." Emmett shook his head, "No sir, Miss Tish, I don't care to get to know that bunch any more than I do." He sighed. Then, after a brief pause, he continued, "And when did you start going to church? I seen you plenty of Sunday mornings out on that horse of yourn and you ain't been wearing any Sunday-go-to-meetin' clothes."

"I understand, Emmett, how you feel. But you know that some of these people need help in ways you don't," she spoke in a whisper. "The town people don't understand the needs out in Crazy Creek. About half the people out there are too proud to accept welfare, but they might accept some services or charity. I know you have found a way to provide for your family, but you must think of the others. You know the money that comes through the government has so many strings attached, I can't even find the ends."

"Oh, all right," Emmett said, "but there ain't no good goin' to come of it. I can promise you that."

Emmett wasn't quite sure how Tish had talked him into entering his bluegrass group into the festival talent contest. He had always agreed to almost everything she asked of him even though he wondered about her sanity at times. He wondered what a pretty little thing like Latisha Jamison was doing wasting her time with a bunch of poor little younguns' who were going to grow up just like their folks before them. He'd heard her talk about education until he thought he would croak, but he kept his children in school just to keep from fussing with her. He'd be better off if he kept Charley home to help with the still. Charley would be better off, too, learning a good trade like making whiskey instead of reading all that foolishness.

Well, here he was on this infernal bus, Emmett thought, he and some of his good neighbors and some of his good-for-nothing neighbors. Some of them looked miserable, sort of like scolded puppies. No one was comfortable going where they knew they weren't wanted. The bus pulled to a halt beside the big stone Central Methodist Church. The passengers piled out looking to Tish for instructions.

"Just go in and find yourselves a seat anywhere you can. There may not be room for you to sit together."

Everyone nodded soberly. Some of the children looked wonderingly at the impressive building, awed by its pentacle pointing toward the heavens. Tish led the way gingerly with the same familiarity she had known when she attended regularly. She walked briskly down the aisle and found a half empty pew. The others followed. Several people squeezed in beside Tish. As she watched the others finding seats, she noticed the odd expressions on the faces in the congregation. When she saw Alex, he averted his eyes embarrassed to recognize her. She bit her lip to keep from laughing. What a jackass!

The sea of faces was just as she had expected, expressions which reflected amazement, curiosity, anger, and, in general, prejudice. Still, she noted, there were also some kind welcoming smiles scattered throughout, those of the good souls who tried earnestly to live their Christian faith.

The choir was standing to sing. There were a few cracked high notes wavering over the others. Mrs. Ayre was performing as usual, weaving as she sang, her voice weaving along with her. Tish felt cold stares at her. Was she imagining it or was it truly a psychic thing that people could really feel such things? She wasn't sure. Just then, the music waned lower and she could hear people whispering behind her.

"What are these people doing here?" someone asked.

"I can't imagine," the answer was hushed, "Look, there's that bootlegger right here in the sheriff's church! The nerve!" The whispering stopped with the end of the hymn.

The minister looked over the packed sanctuary. Just as he was apologizing for the air-conditioning unit being out of order, ladies began to fan themselves. Seeing them reminded Tish of the services held in the old clapboard church up in Crazy Creek. It was still being used without air-conditioning. The minister welcomed the visitors with what appeared to be a forced smile on his face. Perhaps it was because he was expecting some out-of-town dignitaries, not these mountaineers.

"I'll bet that was hard for him," Tish said silently to herself. She knew that these guests were not well-heeled enough financially to suit this particular preacher. He much preferred those affluent newcomers who had sold their homes up North and were flocking to new developments in the South. Some of the fancy gated communities were located on what was once lush farmland confiscated by TVA. The yankees, as local folks referred to them, moved to the Southern states where the climate was warmer and taxes lower. However, some also brought with them their old liberal agendas for yankee-style government which meant taxes were going up in the valley as well.

Tish spotted her friend Marlo as she moved from the organ bench where she had been playing a beautiful arrangement. They exchanged smiles. The minister explained the purpose of the gathering, to pray for a successful fund-raising effort, to bless those who were going to compete, and to enjoy each other in fellowship while conducting such a worthy cause. He also announced that following this prayer service, food vendors were set up on the street and would be selling all kinds of foods for lunch.

More announcements were made followed by a prayer and another hymn. It was a tuneless unfamiliar one. Tish noticed that her group sat silently, just listening. The women were meek in their worn cotton dresses. Ossie Richards wore what was once someone's cocktail dress. She had wanted so much not to embarrass Tish by looking dowdy. Tish could not dispel her pleasure when she had proudly shown the dress that a fine lady had given her. Secretly, Tish had wanted to wallop the fine lady. Why the hell would someone give a cocktail dress to someone like Mrs. Richards who never went further than the tobacco patch. She probably didn't even know what a cocktail was. Who did the fine lady think she was helping?

Mr. and Mrs. Smithers, crowded close together beside Tish, wore rumpled winter clothing. Although the windows were opened all the way, the church was stuffy as the stillness of the air hung heavily on the unseasonably warm day. More than a few of Tish's guests laundered frugally. They thought undue scrubbing weakened the fabric of their garments. But, it was not only the mountain folks who were perspiring; everyone was. Tish knew she had smelled more pleasant odors than those circulating in the air. She was pleased with Emmett in his clean bib overalls and crisp blue shirt. Mattie looked nice too in a cool gingham dress.

Tish noticed gleefully that the Jenkins family was sitting next to her Aunt Ruby in one of the pews closest to the pulpit. Aunt Ruby was smothering in a richly brocaded suit. Tish often wondered if her hands grew tired under the weight of the diamonds she wore. Poor, frail Emma Jenkins, dressed simply and devoid of any jewelry, provided quite a contrast to Aunt Ruby.

The Malone baby started to cry, but not any louder than the minister's baby. Three year-old Sissy Malone took advantage of her mother's fussing over the baby to slide from the pew and wander in the aisle looking at people. Spotting Tish, she ran and climbed into her lap. Tish held the little girl lovingly. This is what her job was all about, Tish thought, a better life for this cuddly little bundle. Sissy burrowed her head into Tish's shoulder and fell fast asleep. The speakers droned on, many saying the same thing as those who had spoken before them; all wanting some credit for planning the contest.

Mercifully, the program was about to come to an end. The minister rose again and quoted the biblical passage, "Where two or three of you are gathered together, there shall I be also." This was followed by the closing hymn., "Shall We Gather at the River," an old hymn familiar to everyone, especially the Crazy Creek folks who always sang it at their baptisms which were held in a quiet pool downstream from the bubbling headwaters. The congregation sang energetically filling the sanctuary with sound. The voices of the rural poor soared above the rest.

People began spilling from the building. Tish moved briskly still holding Sissy Malone. The group converged on the bus to get their box lunches, then settled under the Maple trees in the yard. Children ran and shrieked, playing hide and seek in the shrubs. Members of the church and community stood on the steps and walks, all of them looking at Tish who smiled sweetly, demurely, thinking herself the biggest hypocrite of all. Finally the minister came over and shook a few hands. Marlo stopped on her way to the car; she would like to have stayed if she didn't need a drink so badly. She surmised what Tish was up to and wished she could help. She couldn't; she had to get home.

"Hey, Tish," Julie's voice rang out, "got any extra food?"

"Sure," Tish answered, "fried chicken, pimento cheese, and chocolate cake. And we've got a huge barrel of lemonade."

"Oh, no!" Julie laughed, "not that!" She pointed at an old whiskey barrel originally from the Jack Daniels distillery over in Lynchburg, more currently used by Emmett Moss, but still showing the original Jack Daniels lettering as visible as the day it was new. Tish spread a blanket for them and she and Julie sat down. Some members of the church were clicking their tongues and tying their faces with strange contortions.

"Can you imagine," whispered Agnes Meyer to Mrs. Zickle, "behaving like that here on our beautiful lawn! The nerve of Latisha Jamison bringing in all these trashy people! Lord, help us."

"I thought I was going to be sick during the service,"replied Mrs. Zickle, "the smell of those people.

They never bathe. You just can't help people like that. And to think what I've done for some of them. I gave that beautiful dress to that Richards woman. Just look at it now. She doesn't have any more sense than to wear it to a church and picnic. Oh, how low some people get. I thought it was bad when those black people came from Knoxville, but they, at least, knew how to dress!"

"Knew their prayers and hymns, too," chimed Agnes.

People were hanging around longer than usual. Some of them were worrying about the grass and shrubs. Others were wondering if the bathrooms should be locked. Little Jeff Meyer spotted a friend from school, Jeff Dobbs, who was munching on a piece of cake.

"Hey, Jim," he exclaimed happily. "Boy, am I ever happy to see you. Did you bring your marbles?"

"No, Ma don't let me play on the Sabbath. She knows I gamble with 'em. Want some cake?" Jim held out a large piece of dark chocolate cake dripping thick fudge icing.

"Sure, swell," Jeff exclaimed reaching for the cake. He took a big bite leaving lots of evidence on his chin.

His mother looked around just in time to see the cake in and around his mouth. She shrieked and ran to him.

"Come here this minute!" And as she grabbed his wrist, she forced the cake from his grasp.

"Aww . . . Mom, you made me drop my cake! Why'd you do that for?"

"You are not to eat anything from those trashy people, and I don't want you playing with them either. Do you understand? You can be nice to them, but keep your distance!"

Jeff lowered his head. How the hell were you supposed to be nice to people when you couldn't get close to them. Geez . . . how was he going to shoot marbles with Jim from a distance? He wondered if all grown people were crazy or just his mother.

The church members and onlookers gradually dispersed, leaving the picnickers on the grounds.

The mountain people ate well on Sundays. It was traditionally chicken day. The barrel of lemonade still held a hint of sour mash and teased the taste buds with its faint smell. After the the picnic, Tish made sure everything was picked up. There was not one scrap of litter left, she observed, as everything was loaded again on the bus. There would be a little time left for them to try to relax before the contest began.

They left the bus where it was and walked across the street to the Memorial Building.

"Okay," she told Emmett who was the proclaimed leader of the group, "You all can sit and wait or wander around and look at the vendors, whatever, until the music begins. I'll try to find out when your band will play."

"Darn, Miss Tish, we done left the instruments on

the bus!"

"Well, you've got plenty of time to get them, I think," Tish said.

As Emmett left, Tish went to the registration table to find out when the band would be on.

The lady at the table scanned the list and asked, "What is the name of the group?"

Tish thought for a minute, then said, "I don't know. They were signed up as Emmett Moss, their leader."

The lady looked again, "I see that name out from the blank space where the name of the band is supposed to be, but I need to know that before I can place them in order."

"O.K., put down 'Crazy Creek.'"

When Emmett returned with the instruments and other members of the group, Tish asked what they called themselves.

"We ain't got no name, Miss Tish, We just play for fun."

"Well, you got a name now. It's 'Crazy Creek'; I just named you."

They were given a piece of cardboard with the number twelve printed on it. Tish thought to herself that it was certainly going to be a long day. Suddenly, the speakers blared and people scattered to find their seats and perspective places. The contestants were to line up behind the stage so there should be no delay between acts.

"Good luck!" Tish told Emmett and his fellow

musicians who were grinning with anticipation. They were feeling at ease now that they had their instruments in hand.

Tish sat down, prepared to listen to no telling what. She was pleasantly surprised to find the level of talent quite impressive. Most of the competitors sang popular country or pop songs. She noticed the three judges making notes and wondered who was winning so far. The program moved along fairly quickly with the contestants scurrying on and off the stage. When it was time for Emmett's group, there was a slight pause and Tish feared they might have gotten stage fright and fled. Then, she heard a twang on a guitar string and realized they were tuning their instruments. They entered the stage, quickly took their customary positions and began to play. The song they chose was "Wildwood Flower", a crowd favorite because of it's fast happy stomp-your-feet kind of sound. Emmett played the fiddle, one of his sons strummed a banjo, another fellow was really good on the mandolin and two others played guitars while all of them sang.

The crowd loved it and called for an encore but the rules would not allow any one entry to do more than one selection.

At the end of the day, modest cash prizes were awarded to the first three places. Tish was thrilled that "Crazy Creek" won Second Place. First Place went to a really talented singer and third went to a good quartet. Everyone seemed satisfied and willing to accept the decision of the judges without complaint or criticism.

Although Tish was happy for the winners, she was tired and glad the contest was over. It had been a very long day and would get even longer before she could get home. She was going to have to ride back up the mountain on the old bus to retrieve her own vehicle, then drive home.

Chiding herself, she mumbled to no one in particular, "I should have thought of that and followed the bus." But, if I had, she thought, I wouldn't have been able to travel down memory lane like I did, riding in that old relic.

CHAPTER TWO

Tish, Julie, and Marlo sat around the felt covered table in the game room of the Scott mansion. It was the kind of evening they had shared many times.

"Tish, did anything come of your Saturday outing?" Julie asked as Marlo dealt another hand of three-handed Rook.

"Nothing good," Tish sighed, "unless you count the fact that Alex hasn't spoken to me all week."

Julie threw back her head and laughed. The sound of her laughter was hard to describe; sort of like bells ringing under a waterfall. Marlo smiled, enjoying the sound of Julie's strange laughter as much as Tish's sarcastic humor. Marlo found it difficult to understand why her friends seemed to resent Alex so much since she, personally, considered him very appealing.

"The membership of the church doesn't see my

people any differently than they ever did." Tish had subconsciously adopted the habit of referring to all the rural poor, not just her assigned caseload, as her people. I got several phone calls, mostly curious, just wondering why I brought them to the opening program. I took the calls as an opportunity to try to get someone to pay to fix Myrtle's teeth. Poor little thing is terribly self-conscious and who wouldn't be." Tish paused, then said, "Maybe if I threaten to bring them back every Sunday, I could blackmail the church!"

Julie's laughter echoed through the large room. She sat casually, one foot tucked under her as she made note of her cards. Her olive skin, sleek black hair and brown eyes radiated joy to all those around her. She had the ability to enjoy herself in every single moment of life, no matter how trivial. Julie played her card and quickly ran the deck.

"That puts me over the winning mark," she said triumphantly.

"Listen, you two," Tish explained, "it's not that I don't enjoy your company, but it's getting late and I'm tired. So you won't mind if I call it a night?"

"Spoil sport!" Julie protested.

"At least have a nightcap with us before you go," Marlo pleaded.

"Okay," Tish said looking at Julie who returned her worried expression. Julie and Tish had discussed Marlo's excessive drinking, but had never confronted her.

"Just a little one for me . . . remember, I've got to drive that mountain road," Tish said.

Marlo brought a silver tray from the bar carrying three crystal glasses and placed them on the table, "Cheers," she said, as she raised her glass.

"It's just as well we broke up the card game early," Julie said as she looked at her watch, "I've got a late date with Freddie."

"Oh, it's Freddie again," Marlo teased, "Last week it was Tom, Dick, and Harry!"

"Oh, stop it!" Julie fluttered her eyes, "I'm going to make up my mind real soon. You'll see, I'm going to beat you both to the alter."

The room seemed ominously silent to Marlo after the departure of Tish and Julie. She fixed herself another drink before moving to another room. The mansion was just so large, no wonder she felt so lost and alone, she thought, as she looked about her at the magnificent old walnut furniture, opulent light fixtures, and imported Oriental rugs. She wondered what led her grandparents to build such a place. They, like herself, had certainly loved home, Jensen's Valley and the surrounding mountains; too bad her parents did not.

On the drive home, Tish enjoyed singing along with the radio. The moon was busy stroking the landscape with soft silver lights. When she turned the car onto the road that jutted through the farmland, the tall pine grove enveloped her in darkness. Then, as always, she burst through the tunnel of trees and there stood home, her own little cottage, built on her favorite childhood spot. It was here in this very place where she had played house, making mud pies in jar lids and placing them on old boards above a moss carpet. Then, she would raid the lime pile before it was spread on the fields to make topping for her pies and icing for the mud cakes. Oh, what silly fun it had been. Tish was glad to be home.

The following morning at the Department of Human Services Tish sat at her desk going through the morning mail and savoring the aroma of the brewing coffee. She noticed a familiar envelope and pulled it from the stack. It was from Marlo. Tish ripped into it wondering what Marlo was up to sending her a letter; she didn't mention it last night. The note said simply that the enclosed check was for Myrtle's teeth. Tish tossed the letter to Alex and reached for the phone.

"Marlo," Tish said, "I just got your check. Listen, I wasn't hinting last night when I said I was trying to find someone to pay for Myrtle's dental work. You've already given so much." There was a pause. "I don't care how much money you have, it just doesn't seem right for one person to pay for practically everything." There was another pause. "Well, thanks a million. I'm going to set up an appointment right now. I'll talk to you later. Bye."

Alex had listened to Tish's side of the conversation carefully. When she put the receiver down, he spoke to Tish for the first time since Saturday, "Tish, I wish you wouldn't try to talk people out of giving money. You know we need every penny we can get. The government barely covers our operating expenses." He grew increasingly redder in the face as he always did when he was angry.

"You spoke to Marlo about fairness . . . well, do you think it's fair that she has more money than any broad in the state? And what's she ever done to earn it? Not a damn thing except strut her glorious ass around."

Tish wanted to slap his face. Mabel's face became crimson, she knew that Marlo and Tish were close friends. She found Alex insufferable.

Tish glared at Alex then spoke directly to the secretary, "Mabel, do you think the coffee's ready?" She knew that nothing irritated Alex more than being ignored, especially when he was in the mood to bully the staff. He had always been a bully, even as a child, making poor Davy Moss's life miserable in school. Guess he was always going to be an ass, Tish thought.

Tish made home visits for the rest of the day. Finally, she went home, showered away the dirt and grime which she had accumulated during the humid day and put on shorts and a tee shirt. Although it was late in the evening, the temperature hadn't dropped. She stretched out on the sofa to watch television, but quickly fell asleep. Several hours passed before she was awakened by the low growl of her little terrier. Listening, she didn't hear anything but the dog leaped up and began barking viciously, running back and forth from Tish to the door. Tish moved swiftly across the room and picked up the shotgun she kept in the corner. She sat down, silently pulling back the hammer, praying. She would not hesitate for an instant to fire if anyone entered. From where she stood, she knew she could cover all entrances, including the windows. She hushed the dog; he obeyed reluctantly. She heard the footsteps on the patio. One good thing about a shotgun, she thought, she wouldn't have to take very good aim. The footsteps stopped. The dog began snarling and growling. "Listen!" Tish commanded in a whisper.

"Miss Tish," a man's voice called, "it's Jason Webb."

Tish sighed in relief but was seized by a sudden shiver. Something must have happened up in the knobs to have brought Jason, "What's the matter, Jason?" Tish unlatched the door.

"Miss Tish, there's big trouble." Jason's voice gave way to the fear he felt. "Ever since you took the busload to the town church, people been kiddin' the sheriff, sayin' how old Emmett's gotten mighty uppity since he got the law under his thumb. You never heard the like of hogwash people been givin' Sheriff Tompkins. They're all askin' him how much Emmett's payin' him to keep the lid on his still."

Everything was clearing for Tish. The truth of the matter was that all of the known moonshiners in the county were paying, one way or another, Sheriff Tompkins . . .everyone but Emmett Moss. All Emmett ever gave the sheriff was a few quarts of his product. He was very proud of the fact that he never bribed the law with money, not considering the liquor anything more than a token of his appreciation for the lack of intervention in his business. Emmett had never seen anything wrong with selling whiskey. If there was anything wrong, it was the meddling of the government. If they worked as hard on folks' real troubles, they wouldn't have time nor interest in what folks were drinking.

Jason caught his breath and started talking again, "Miss Tish, some of them folks in the town say they're going to get themselves another sheriff since he's taken to worshippin' with moonshiners."

There was going to be hell to pay, thought Tish, and it was all her fault. Tish Jamison, the do-gooder. "Where'd you hear all this. Jason?"

He pushed his hands into his overall pockets and said, "In the pool hall. Me and Ralph was playing for pocket money over at the corner table so they didn't pay us any mind. Miss Tish, I'm really scared."

Tish noticed that he was trembling. "Sit down while I think. Try to get hold of yourself," She watched as he sank into the nearest chair. The oldest of the Webb children, Jason had grown into a towering mass of muscles during his nineteen years. It was disconcerting to see him shaking so. Although he had dropped out of school after the eighth grade, he had kept the local library busy and went through the best novels on their shelves. Tish noticed however, that his speech was understandably still patterned after that of his neighbors.

"What do you think they're going to do? Are you worried about the men in the pool hall or the sheriff or what, Jason?"

"One of the sheriff's cousins was in there, hearin' the talk and he told the others to stop their fussing because Tompkins was a fixin' to do a raid. You know the men out home will try to protect themselves and I'm afraid somebody will get shot."

Now, Tish was also afraid. Jason made perfect sense.

"How'd you get here?" suddenly Tish remembered she hadn't heard a car.

"Bessie."

"The mule!" Tish gasped. "You must be exhausted; here, drink this." Tish handed him a tumbler of bourbon. She poured another for herself, noticing the look of surprise in Jason's eyes. She was upset, it never occurred to her that Jason might not drink. He had, in fact, been raised on whiskey, commonly used in most of the mountain homes for medicinal purposes. Jason's surprise sprang from the fact that Tish drank. For some reason, he assumed that all social workers would be above the need, certainly the desire.

"Do you have any idea when they're going to raid?"

"Right at dawn."

"Oh, dear Lord, we haven't got much time." Tish was looking at the wall clock as it began to chime. "I napped longer than I realized. Does Emmett know about the raid?"

"Yes, me and Ralph left the pool hall and went straight out there to tell him first thing. He said he's going to kill whatever son-of-a-bitch comes near his still. Miss Tish, he means it, that's why I'm so scared."

Tish swallowed hard. She wasn't worried about Sheriff Tompkins. It was concern for Emmett and his family that gripped her. Emmett, always too proud to take any kind of government assistance, had said he'd never take food stamps like some sorry egg-sucking dog. He'd either be killed or hauled off to jail.

"It's past midnight, but we've got time."

"For what, Miss Tish?" Jason looked up bewildered.

"We'll move the still."

"Where? They'll look all over the knobs. I don't know of any other hiding places."

"We'll take it out of the knobs and bring it here," Tish exclaimed.

"You're kiddin,' here in your house!"

"Well, just for tonight, anything to prevent a killing!"

"How are we going to move it? They'd spot Emmett's truck and we sure can't get it all in your
Ranchero." Jason was stumped.

Tish tossed her long brown hair and raised an
eyebrow at Jason as if to imply that the answer was
obvious, "You said you rode Bessie over here. So,
we'll kill two birds with one stone by using my
horse trailer; first to take Bessie home, then, on the
return trip, to bring the still here. The trailer's got a
removable center partition. I think it'll work just fine. While she was talking, she was gathering her
keys, putting on her boots and making preparations
to leave.

"Let's go!"

Jason and Tish got into her Ranchero and moved
cautiously through the field taking a new, less con-
spicuous route to the barn. It would not be good for
her parents who lived nearby to see car lights approaching the barn at this hour of the night. As they
neared the barn lot, Tish cut off the lights, feeling
gratitude for the moonlight. Like thieves, they
hooked up the trailer and returned slowly to the cottage to pick up Bessie.

"I'm really glad we have Bessie here to make it
look good." Tish was beginning to enjoy herself.

"She ain't never been loaded before," warned Jason.

"There's a first time for everything, or so I've
been told." Tish said with more optimism than she

felt. They removed Bessie's bridle and put a halter on her and led her to the back of the trailer. "Come on, Bessie," Tish stepped into the trailer but Bessie refused to move. Tish pulled firmly, Bessie pulled back planting her legs firmly, defiantly.

"It's no use, Miss Tish, she's powerful stubborn." Jason said.

"Let's don't give up yet," Tish said, hoping Jason was as strong as he looked. She ran the lead rope through the feed slot at the front of the trailer and pulled it around the hitch.

"Now, Jason, let's stand a little to the side and put our arms behind her rump and push. I've seen this done and it usually works. Just be careful,"

They must have surprised the mule because she lunged into the trailer looking somewhat bewildered. They were giddy.

"Gee, Miss Tish, I never thought I'd see the day when old Bessie'd be ridin' around in a fancy horse trailer." Jason laughed.

"I never thought I'd be hauling' a moonshine still either." They both laughed. There was no way to avoid going through town to get to the road leading to the knobs and Crazy Creek. Hopefully, everyone would be sleeping.

"Uh oh," Jason warned, "Look behind you."

As Tish looked, she saw the patrol car turn on its blinking red light. Not having broken any traffic rules, Tish couldn't imagine why she was being pulled over. She stopped and watched as the officer approached her.

"Miss Jamison, you haven't got any lights on your horse trailer."

Hell, Tish thought, in the rush, she'd forgotten to hook up the lights. There was a plug near the hitch.

"Gee, Officer Mercer, thanks for telling me. I didn't know, I'll get them fixed right away."

"You just getting home from a horseshow?" he asked.

Tish started to lie and agree with his assumption. Apparently he hadn't noticed that she was headed in the wrong direction to be going home. Just then, Bessie began to bray as only a mule can. There was no way to avoid offering some explanation. If she told him she had been to a show, he'd make a big deal out of her showing a mule. Jason was beginning to fidget as the mule kept on braying.

"No, sir, I haven't been to a show. Jason's mother is sick and Jason came out on the mule to get me. I'm just taking her home as I go. I'm going to see what I can do for his mother." Tish thought it best to tell as much of the truth as possible.

"Why Jason," Officer Mercer said, "I'd have driven you out to get Miss Jamison if you had stopped by the jail."

Jason nodded his appreciation.

"Hope your mother gets better real soon," Officer Mercer said as he waved them on.

Tish wondered why he had looked at her with such confusion because he seemed to believe her story. Hurriedly, they continued to drive.

"The whole place is dark," Jason said as they pulled up at Emmett's house. "Reckon we ought to wake him up before we do anything."

The shed door cracked exposing a sliver of glow from a lantern. After Emmett recognized them, he pushed the door aside. They could see a gleaming gun barrel at his side.

"Lord have mercy, what in thunder are you doing out here in the middle of the night? Miss Tish, you should be ashamed of yourself running around in short pants!" Emmett was scolding.

"We're going to move your still," Tish answered, ignoring his remarks.

"No, sir, I'm sick and tired of runnin' and hidin' with it every time some sorry sheriff gets his dander up. Too damn bad if they can't realize I'm savin' the government money by makin' myself a livin'. If that sheriff can't see that, he's just plain stupid," Emmett was riled.

"We have to move the still." Tish spoke with determination, "If you go and shoot somebody, what's going to happen to Mattie and the children? You know they'll catch you and haul you off to jail. It'll be on my conscience because I was the one who got the sheriff all fired up by taking you to his church. Jason, unload Bessie and start loading this stuff." Tish didn't wait for Emmett's reaction before taking action. He looked at her helplessly for a few minutes before helping them dismantle portions of the still. Tish backed the trailer part way into the shed so they could load more quickly. After loading the main pot, they followed with the thump keg and finally a barrel of mash. Boxes of moonshine were packed wherever space could be found.

"I'm getting out of here," Tish said, "I'm so tired, I'm going to leave all this stuff in the driveway tonight. If they catch me with it, I don't much care as long as they give me a place to sleep." She smiled wryly, trying to keep a positive attitude although she was really afraid she might get caught.

Tish felt a rough hand touch her tenderly on the shoulder. She saw tears in Emmett's eyes. There was no need for words. She jumped into the driver's seat and was off.

She drove as fast as she dared noticing that the sky was beginning to brighten with first light. She was almost at the intersection of the main road when she passed the sheriff's car which was being followed closely by several other vehicles. Officer Mercer waved. As the distance between them grew, so did a feeble sense of security grow inside Tish. The rest of the trip was a blur. She pulled into her driveway, fell into her bed and was fast asleep before the red sky rose completely over the horizon to light up the day.

A phone was ringing somewhere in the distance. Tish pulled a pillow down over her ears. The irritating sound continued, growing louder as wakefulness overcame her. Crawling from the bed, she realized that she was still wearing clothes. The strange smell that had penetrated her sleep, she now recognized as sour mash. She stumbled toward the phone. "Hello."

"Don't tell me you're still in bed," it was her mother's voice.

"Well, yes, I was."

"I just wanted to tell you that lunch is on the table, in case you would like some. I've made a big pot of vegetable soup." Rebecca Jamison had just offered Tish an irresistible bribe to her daughter's appetite.

"I'll be right over as soon as I get dressed. Don't wait. I'll help myself when I get there."

Now, fully awake, she remembered the still. What the heck, she thought, I'm famished. If the still's been sitting there in the driveway in broad daylight all morning, it can just sit there for an hour or two more. After feeding her patient little dog and giving him some hugs and affectionate words, she peeled off her odorous clothing and jumped hurriedly into the shower. She put on jeans and walked outside while buttoning her blouse.

When she approached the trailer, she noticed that the tops of the barrels were visible, their rims gleaming in the sunlight. She went back into the house, got a couple of blankets and carefully covered the cargo. Then, she jogged the familiar path through the woods with her dog at her heels. As she let herself in the kitchen door, she noticed her family had waited lunch for her.

"I told you not to wait," she said.

"We didn't mind. We look forward to having a weekend meal with our daughter. You know, you're so busy through the week we don't see you often enough."

"And you're probably worn out," her grandmother chimed in, "looking out for all those folks you see about up there in Crazy Ceek."

There was a knock on the door. It was Uncle Jack. Tish's mother set a place for him as the others continued their meal.

Uncle Jack cleared his throat loudly, as he always did when he was about to announce some big news.

"Did you hear about the raid?" he asked triumphantly, knowing they probably hadn't.

"No, what kind of raid? Everyone but Tish asked at once.

"That fool sheriff took about 30 men out to the Moss place early this morning. He even took the newspaper man with him. Said he knew for a fact that Emmett had a still and he knew where to find it. Old Mac Wilson was along too. He said it was the funniest thing he'd ever seen happen. Old Mac said he was riding in the car with the sheriff and the newspaper man, just listening and watching. He said he didn't know why they wanted him to go with them unless maybe they thought they might need a witness or something. He said the sheriff was bragging to the newsman that they were going to bust up the biggest moonshine operation in East Tennessee. He warned them to be careful because the Moss gang would be armed and dangerous."

Uncle Jack interrupted himself to ask for another piece of cornbread. No one had noticed that Tish had stopped eating.

"Well sir," Uncle Jack continued, they stopped the cars about a hundred yards or so from Emmett's place. Everything was dark. They were congratulating themselves on how successful they had been in planning a surprise attack. They went creeping in like varmints after chickens, down on all fours. Some of them were so scared, they were trembling. The newspaper man got his camera all focused while the sheriff and some others shoved open the shed door. And, bless Pat, there wasn't a thing in the shed except a pile of logs." Everyone laughed; Uncle Jack, loudest of all.

"Well sir," he was warming to his story, "the sheriff was so mad, he was fit to be tied. He went storming up to the house pounding on the door loud enough to wake the dead. Old Emmett came to the door in his night shirt, just as polite as you please, inviting everyone in for coffee. The sheriff stomped around and started yelling at Emmett, wanting to know where the hell the still was. Emmett, still being just as polite as you please, told the sheriff, 'Why, sheriff, I thought you knowed I done sold my operation to a man up in Sevier County. It's one of them on display in the fed's land up there . . .

you know, up there by the national park where they got that tourist town, Gatlinburg. There was just too much competition around here what with this wide open county we got, thanks to you, of course.'

"The sheriff, according to Mac, turned as red as a pickled beet and everybody, even the deputies bust our laughing." Uncle Jack punched the table.

"Is it true that Emmett stopped his operation?" Tish's father, Charles Jamison, asked as the laughter subsided.

"I don't know, but Mac said he bought a quart from Emmett early yesterday right there in the shed with the pot bubbling. Nobody can figure out how Emmett got the still and all that 'shine out of there. His truck was setting on blocks, not a tire on it. And they'd been watching the road for days. They stopped every truck out of there for the past two days. Today, they're out combing the woods all around the Moss place. They searched his house last night and early this morning, it was just about day-break. They said old Emmett was just sitting on his big porch rocking and chewing tobacco like he did-n't have a care in the world."

"Here's dessert," Tish's mother began passing around dishes filled with hot blackberry cobbler topped with fresh whipped cream. Tish ate hers quickly before excusing herself from the table. She filled the sink with steaming sudsy water and began washing the dishes. Charles Jamison walked with Uncle Jack outside to sit in the yard. Tish finished the dishes as quickly as possible and told everyone goodbye. They were used to her comings and goings and hardly noticed her leaving.

She was nervous about having the still in her driveway. Hurriedly, she jogged the path home and immediately rushed to check the horse trailer. It was empty! Oh, Lord, she thought, did the sheriff find it or someone else? Her family would be disgraced. She would lose her job. Sinking to the ground, about to cry, Tish noticed a piece of paper stuck on the back door. She grabbed for it.

"Everything is taken care of. Thanks, Jason." the note read.

Tish sighed deeply, She had no idea where or how Jason had moved it, but she was certainly glad it was gone. Then, remembering the bottles inside the Ranchero, some behind the seat, some under the seat, more in a big box in the passenger seat, she unlocked the vehicle and began unloading. She certainly didn't want to have a wreck, even a fender bender, with her car all loaded with moonshine. She put some of the bottles under her bed, some in the closet, and the rest in cabinets and drawers. Finally, after finding more nooks and crannies in her house than she knew existed, all the bottles were out of sight.

CHAPTER THREE

Summer seemed to sneak from Jensen's Valley without anyone noticing its departure, leaving shorter cooler days in its wake. Marlo and Julie held Tish's birthday celebration indoors for the first time. Always before, the traditional early September outing had been held around the pool at the Scott estate. This September birthday celebration signaled what would become an unusually cold autumn with its chill winds already hurrying the leaves into changing colors.

Marlo was always reminded of her own birthday which would follow Tish's in December, only hers would mark the end of more years. Julie and Tish were the same age, Julie having arrived in May, four months before Tish. Marlo, on the other hand, had already been on earth as a living, breathing person for nearly five years before the births of her friends.

She was beginning to feel very old. She decided that 28 was indeed a long time to live unhappily and alone. Pensive, she watched Julie and Tish chattering over the gigantic cake filled with candles. She doubted that either of them had ever spent a lonely day in their entire lives.

"Margaret, you really outdid yourself today, the food was scrumptious!" Julie was addressing the loyal servant of the Scott household.

Margaret grinned, "Thank you, dear. It was my pleasure to make it special." She planned the birthday event for the three girls with as much care as she gave to the huge dinner parties hosted by the older Scotts when they were in the valley. In fact, there was nothing Margaret wouldn't do for Marlo. It was only because of Marlo's insistence that she came to the mansion only three times each week instead of everyday as she did when the older Scotts were there. Although she appreciated having more time to herself, she could not help but worry about her young charge. To Margaret, Marlo would forever be a little girl.

Each birthday was celebrated with the enthusiasm of youngsters who refused to grow up. In a way, the three girls shared a sisterhood of sorts. Marlo had been born to the Scotts late in life, after they had given up hope of having children and were resigned to being childless. Because of it, she had been over-protected, even more than the average wealthy child. She had been educated in private boarding schools giving her little chance to develop friendships in her own community. She had gotten to know Julie and Tish through horseback riding since her horse was boarded in the stables owned and operated by Julie's grandfather. Julie was also an only child, having been left under the care of her grandparents at an early age. Tish, although a sister to two other girls, was so much younger that she was unable to play with them during her childhood. In fact, they had proven to be a hindrance, tattle-telling on her at every turn and forever complaining that she was messing up their lives by her very existence. They had always hated it when she went into their room and played dress-up in their teenage clothes and make-up.

Julie and Marlo did seem more like sisters to her, or at least what she thought sisters should be. She sometimes remarked about what a strange socio-economic team they made; one rich, one poor, and the other poorer. But, in truth, none of them were poor. It was just that Marlo was so rich, everyone else seemed poor by comparison. Yet, they had never been jealous of all the things Marlo had and she knew for certain that it was not her money that made them like her.

They shrieked in delight as Margaret entered the room with a serving tray carrying yet another special treat. Now, it was something in flames. "Beautiful! Oh, Margaret, you're spoiling us!"

"Haven't I always?" Margaret retorted.

Finally, after eating all they could possibly hold, they spent the rest of the afternoon sharing old experiences.

"Do you remember how we felt the first time we saw Marlo?" Julie asked Tish, throwing a teasing glance at Marlo.

"Yes," Tish giggled. "We were riding over by Pa's stable and there she was, right out of the storybook." Everyone in Jensen's Valley called Julie's grandfather 'Pa'. "Marlo, do you still have your first little riding habit?" Tish remembered how impressed she had been. It was the first time she had ever seen anyone dressed in hunting attire. She and Julie had been helping Pa spread wood shavings in the freshly cleaned stalls. It was the perfect chore for five year olds who delighted in the task. In had walked Marlo dressed in kaiki colored jodhpurs, a smart black coat, tall boots, and a velveteen helmet. Her blond curls were pinned in a bun at the nap of her neck. She was wearing black riding gloves and carrying a little crop with a popper on the end of it. The scarf around her neck was fastened with a gold pin shaped into a bar of stirrups. Julie had pointed wide-eyed at the young stranger who was accompanied by a black man wearing a white jacket. Nine-year old Marlo had smiled at the two little girls. After her ride in the ring on her show pony, she had begged the servant to let her help with the shavings. Yes, Tish remembered, the beginning of their long friendship was clear in her mind's eye.

"Oh, I doubt if I still have it, but there's so much old stuff packed away in this big old house, it could be here somewhere," Marlo laughed. She remembered how envious she had been of the two little girls playing in the barn. Though the three became fast friends, she would never be the friend of Julie or Tish that they were to each other.

The afternoon passed enjoyably. Marlo discovered that several hours passed without her feeling the need for a drink. That realization gave her a feeling of relief. Then everyone left; first, Julie and Tish, then the servants. Marlo found the house uncomfortably quiet, she found the bottle of Scotch tucked in a shoe bag in her closet. She had grown so tired of hearing Margaret complain about her excessive drinking, she had started keeping a few extra bottles hidden away so they wouldn't be missed from the bar. Pouring the Scotch over ice, she wondered when it was that she had stopped using a jigger to measure.

At the piano she began playing Bach. She was grateful that her parents had insisted on music lessons when she was only four. Back then, she had hated the hours of practice. Now, music seemed to be the only solace she could find other than the glass so familiar in her hand. Playing kept her from drinking quite as fast as she otherwise did. She was not sure how long she played. Finally, she noticed that even the notes were beginning to blur. She left the piano to stretch out on the sofa. A short time later, she heard the ringing of the front doorbell. Eagerly she walked to the door, feeling a little unsteady on her feet. Opening the door, she saw that her visitor was Alex Morgan.

"What a surprise, Alex. Do come in," She was gracious as usual.

Alex experienced a sense of relief at Marlo's unexpected welcoming charm. She seemed genuinely glad to see him. He didn't realize that she would have been equally glad to see almost anyone. He followed her into the music room where she offered him a drink. He accepted, feeling more enthusiasm for his mission. He had always found her provocative as the most gorgeous woman he had ever seen off a movie screen. In fact, he thought to himself, she could have become a movie star if she wanted to be.

"Marlo, I hope you don't mind my coming unannounced. I have so many calls to make, I thought I'd just take a chance on catching you home." Alex decided to plunge right in with the purpose of his visit. Once that was out of the way, he's see what else he could make of her hospitality.

"Certainly," Marlo commented, not really caring why he had come. It was good to know that at least someone outside her small group of friends knew she was alive. Also, unless she was imagining it, she could feel his interest in her too.

"I hate to burden you with what I am about to ask, especially since you have always been so helpful to our poor. But, I've been appointed as a trustee for our little church college. Naturally, since you are a Methodist, you know all about it. Well, it's the time of year when we are all asked to make contributions. Uh, I know your parents always have done so in the past, but I thought since they are in Florida, I would talk to you instead. Now, if you aren't interested, I could write them." Alex cleared his throat. He knew all too well that they would be written to anyway by standard form letter mailed to all former contributors to the college.

"How much do they usually give?" Marlo asked.

"I'm not really sure, but, as you know, they are very generous." Alex answered, trying to put as much charm in his voice as possible.

"I have an idea, Alex. Why don't I set up a scholarship for students interested in music? I did that at my own alma mater. I would like the money to go to talented students who could not otherwise attend college."

"Marlo, there are many federal loans available to underprivileged students. What the college really needs is money to spend on basic operations." Alex said.

"I don't care. There is a big difference between a gift and a loan. I want my money to be a gift to someone who loves music as much as I do. I would like it divided among several recipients . . . and " Marlo was becoming enthusiastic about her idea, "I want to have a hand in the selection of the students."

"Very well," Alex frowned, realizing how much more difficult it was going to be to have a portion of this money channeled in the direction of his needs. He had been successfully skimming a little money for himself through his reimbursed expenditures like travel, gas, postage, etc. He had been very cautious with the amounts and was happy with just a little here and there, nothing to arouse suspicion. Sighing, he decided not to worry because there would be other donations. Alex watched Marlo get up and walk to the wall safe in the adjoining room. He saw now in the way she walked just how much the Scotch had affected her. He restrained himself from getting up although he certainly would have liked to be close enough to catch a glimpse of the contents of the safe. As Marlo walked back into the room carrying a checkbook, Alex studied her with a mixture of envy and adoration. She was unbelievably beautiful, rich and charming. More importantly, she possessed everything he wished he had been born with. She didn't have to lift a finger to be special. Bitch, he thought, why could he not have been as lucky?

"Here you go, Alex. I made it out for $10,000. That's just for starters. I need to consult with my accountant and advisers about the best way to go about setting up the scholarship before I give anymore."

Alex tucked the check carefully into his wallet before sinking back comfortably into the plush sofa, very glad that Marlo was pouring him another drink. He wondered what Marlo was thinking because she seemed to be enjoying his company. He had always been popular with girls before he married, he thought as he recalled those fun, carefree days; just maybe he could make her forget that he was married. Or, maybe she wouldn't care, some women didn't.

As the evening progressed, Alex noticed that Marlo was becoming more and more tipsy. He also found her more than receptive to his charming banter. When he finally ventured coming on to her, reaching over and grasping her, she did not push him away. It was hard to believe, he thought. She had everything, why was she so lonely, so giving? He was too selfish for the why . . . he was a taker, not a giver.

For her part, Marlo found the Scotch had subdued her sense of right and wrong; all she could feel was need and desire. Somehow, without intending to yield to his seduction, she allowed her baser emotions to rein. When he reached for her, looking into her eyes, she melted into his arms and was his for the taking.

.

CHAPTER FOUR

Autumn rushed into the valley as hurriedly as the summer had arrived. It had been both a busy but fun-filled summer for Tish who had spent much of her time with the people who lived in the cabins in the Crazy Creek community. Her education in folklore and mountain ways was was growing as she helped make molasses from sugar cane, observed the process of drying fruit under the windows of old cars, stirred fat into lard in an outdoor kettle, and strung yards of green beans to make what was called leather britches. No one could tell her why they were called that, only that they were. On several occasions, she and Julie had attended square dances up on the ridge where a huge flat rock shelf jutted from the side of the mountain. Lanterns were hung from tree limbs to assist the moon in lighting the limestone floor. They enjoyed the fleeting bow of Mac Wilson's fiddle and the rhythm of the man who called the dances. Tish was awed by the ease of those who clogged those ancient moves. When she tried to learn, her feet did not cooperate with her intentions and, laughingly, she stopped trying and just watched.

Julie, as usual, had a grand time. Everyone shouted to her and most wanted to dance with her or introduce her to someone else who did. The mountain people were a little less forward towards Tish. Ever since she had helped hide Emmett's still, they had been awe struck by how far she would go to look out for the people here.

It was the ninth day of November when Tish climbed out of bed to discover the season's first snow. Gazing from the window in childish wonder, she turned on the coffee pot and waited impatiently for the stimulation it promised. The fence posts had become pedestals for little mounds of snow. Tish put on heavy socks and drank her coffee quickly, enjoying the warmth it carried inside. At least she would have hot feet, she thought, as she pulled fleece-lined boots over the thick socks. She found a heavy jacket in the corner of the closet and pulled a toboggan over her ears. Her feet crunched in the deep white carpet as her dog jumped and yelped in delight. Tish ran and jumped also, just as she had as a child. Sometimes she felt as though she still wasn't quite grown up. It was still snowing. She turned her face up toward the sky and felt the big soft flakes pelt her face and catch in her full eyelashes. It was like being in a wonderland, she thought. As she approached the barn, she heard the familiar neighing.

"Are you hungry?" she called to the horses. "Just a minute more." She always talked to them as she scooped grain into their feed buckets. Climbing into the loft, she noticed that snow was blowing in through the cracks in the barn powdering some of the hay. After she had thrown abundant portions of the rich Timothy and Orchard Grass hay into the stalls, she broke the ice on the water tanks. It was a thin layer, not the solid thick covering which would occur later in the winter when the temperatures tended to plunge low and last for days at a time. Then, she would have to carry water unless she bought one of those new-fangled heating gadgets which she was afraid of, for fear it might somehow break and electrocute one of the horses. With the feeding done, Tish decided she would go to her parents house and invite herself to breakfast.

The kitchen was full of warm smells of frying ham, hot bread and coffee. The fireplace held a busy fire.

"Good morning, dear," Rebecca Jamison greeted her daughter. "You're just in time for breakfast."

"I know," grinned Tish, "why do you think I came this early?" She put her arm around her mother's shoulders. "Is it alright if I use the 4-wheel drive truck today? I need to go out to the Ramsey's."

"For crying out loud, LaTisha, on a day like today, I would think you would stay in! Rebecca used

Tish's complete first name only when she needed to make a point.

"I have too many things to see about," Tish was emphatic.

"Well, if you are bent and determined, then by all means use the truck, otherwise, you'll slide off the road. It will still be dangerous though, even in the truck."

"Thanks, Mom. Where's Dad?"

"Still asleep. He stayed up nearly all night working on a case."

Tish thought about her father. He was a typical country lawyer in many ways. Unlike the attorneys in firms in cities who specialized in one form of law or another, Charles did it all. Sometimes it was a simple civil matter; other times, a major criminal case. However, he seemed to enjoy the unusual cases the most. Perhaps, it was because they presented more of a challenge. Tish wasn't sure; she just knew she was proud of him.

Tish looked at her mother, thinking she was still a beautiful woman. "I sure am lucky to have parents with such great genes, smarts from Daddy and looks from you!"

"What you really mean is that you're lucky we never say 'no'." Rebecca gave her daughter a half-kidding, half-scolding look and winked.

"Also, I like your cooking!" Tish said as Rebecca put hot biscuits on the table.

As they sat down and began eating breakfast,

Rebecca asked, "Why do you have to go out to the Ramsey's?"

"Well, you know how cold it's been lately. Yesterday while I was over at the Meadow School checking to see if all the kids had coats, I walked into one of the rooms and saw little Zeke barefoot. I went out immediately and bought him some shoes, socks, and a coat. Oh, Mom, you should have seen his face light up. I figure the whole family must need some help. You see, they're new to the valley. They came from down around Soddy Daisy somewhere. I understand they are squatting in one of the abandoned buildings on T.V.A. Land."

"Well, honey, remember to be diplomatic. You know how much pride some people have."

"Don't worry, Mom, I'm getting real clever about getting people to accept help. It is funny, though, so many of the ones who need the most are the ones who don't want any help. Some of the others who aren't so bad off have always got their hands out."

Tish had trouble getting the truck started. Finally, the engine began to clutter a deep churning noise which eventually gave way to a roar. Tish drove into the unspoiled snow. When she turned onto the main road, she noticed other automobiles with chains making clinking noises. One car, having skidded into a ditch, had been abandoned. Tish shuddered when she arrived at the old Harlow shack. Until recently, it had been used to store corn and other grains for cattle on the farm. The government agency, theTennessee Valley Authority, had taken the entire Harlow farm in a forced sale for another dam, this time on the Little Tennessee River. The big house and all the timber had already been torn down by giant machines which had ravaged the once picturesque country side. Although some of the farm was being leased to farmers, much of it lay fallow and unattended as the Tennessee Valley Authority, better known by the initials, TVA, made plans to sell it to wealthy developers. Some of the landowners, environmentalists, fisherman, and history buffs had organized to try to save the Little T, as the river was referred to, and had managed to halt completion of the project which was the 29th hydroelectric dam to be constructed by TVA. The Ramsey's had moved into an old storage shack with no knowledge of how long they could stay unnoticed or unchallenged by employees of TVA. Some were sympathetic to squatters while others were not. Tish walked to the door which hung on rusty hinges and sported large cracks between the boards. Tish noticed that there was no glass in any of the windows. Cardboard had been nailed across them to block the wind.

"Hello, anybody home?" Tish yelled. A frail woman opened the door. Her eyes were fearful, she said nothing.

"Mrs. Ramsey," Tish said, "I'm Tish Jamison. I know your little boy, Zeke. I thought I'd come out to see him since there's no school today." Tish watched as the Ramsey woman opened the door for her. There was only one room. A feeble blaze burned uselessly in an old pot-bellied stove. The room was dark and cold. Three children huddled together on a bare mattress with one ragged quilt wrapped around them. Zeke was sitting by the stove with his coat on. A wide grin darted across his face when he saw Tish. Mrs. Ramsey was wearing a thin, short sleeved cotton dress.

"Sit down, Miss Jamison," she said.

Tish looked for a place to sit. There was only the mattress, a table and three straight chairs. She sat in one of the chairs. "I wanted to make sure Zeke got home with his shoes."

"Oh yes," Mrs. Ramsey said. Her voice brightened, "He's so proud of them. Why, he even slept with them last night. He said he was afraid somebody might sneak in and steal them. They are the only shoes he's ever had."

Tish felt tears starting. She tucked her head. Mrs. Ramsey was staring bleakly at the stove and didn't notice.

"Listen, I'd like to help you." Tish said abruptly. "Tell me how."

"Lord only knows," Mrs. Ramsey sighed. "My old man . . . ain't no good. I can't leave him 'cause I got nowhere to go. I was 15 when I met him. My folks were what you call migrant workers. We were up in North Carolina pickin' apples when me and

Clyde run off to get married. That was 10 years ago." Tish was shocked to learn that the tired body sitting across from her was only 25 years old.

"Where are your people now?" Tish asked.

"I don't know. Last I heard, they had gone down to Georgia to pick peaches. They were glad to get shed of me. I never was too strong. Guess I was a burden to 'em."

"Is your husband out of work?"

"Yes, he's most always out of work. He sold firewood for a spell but not anymore. All the wood is gone for miles around this place. I've been scratchin' around for brush but them machines didn't leave none."

"Where's your husband now?" Tish asked.

"I don't know."

"Do you have any food?"

"No. I cooked the last of the beans I had day before yesterday."

"Listen," Tish said, "you don't have to live like this. There are emergency food stamps. It may be tomorrow before I get through all the red tape, but I'll see that you have something to eat." Mrs. Ramsey looked puzzled. "I'm a social worker, Mrs. Ramsey; it's my job to help people who are down on their luck."

Tish left the shack in despair. She wondered if she should have explained to the woman that she would be eligible for welfare if she kicked her husband out. This time it might be the best thing to do, but not always. Some of the husbands were good men who, at times, simply could not provide. Damn the stupid system!

Walking into the office, Tish reached for the phone. She called the president of the Woman's Club to suggest they have a load of coal or wood delivered out to the shack to avoid having to place the children in foster care. The Club had a fund for just such emergencies. They agreed. She arranged for food stamps to be processed immediately . She was beginning to feel little surges of hope as she drove back to the Ramsey's with a box of food. She noticed that a large pile of coal had already been delivered. She was thankful for all the generous people who lived in that part of the valley. The Woman's Club was top notch, she thought.

On the way home, Tish stopped to do some barn chores so she wouldn't have to come out in the cold again. As soon as she reached her cottage, she built a fire in the fireplace and made hot chocolate. No sooner had she lifted the mug to her lips than the phone rang.

"Hello," Tish said angrily, not wanting to be disturbed.

"Tish," a woman's voice began. It was Mrs. Atchley, president of the Woman's Club.

"Do you know what that man did?" she was livid.

"What man?"

"That Ramsey!"

"No, what?"

"He sold the coal. Every last chunk of it is gone! He sold it to buy whiskey, got drunk and started running around out there in the fields like a crazy man. The oldest child walked all the way into town and told the sheriff. The rescue squad is out there now looking for him. The temperature has already dropped to five degrees. It's going to keep on dropping. They expect he'll freeze to death before morning."

"Oh, hell." Tish muttered.

"What did you say?"

"Nothing. Thank you so much for calling. I'll get in touch with my supervisor so he can get the kids out of there. He's the only one with enough clout to get them some place to stay tonight."

Tish dialed Alex and explained what had happened.

"Okay, Tish. I'll line up some foster homes. If the family won't budge voluntarily, I'll see to it that the legal work is taken care of so we can take them by force. What about the woman?"

"If you can't find anyplace else to take her, bring her here. I wouldn't leave any living thing out there in this weather without heat, let alone a human being. And, Alex, being in that shack is about the same as being out in the open, it just has cardboard nailed over the windows."

"All right, Tish, I promise I'll take care of it."

Tish hung up the phone, exhausted. She was

relieved that Alex had been so understanding for a change. She drank some more hot chocolate and went to bed. She was too tired to eat.

The Rescue Squad did not find Ramsey that night. The temperature dropped to eight below zero. Everyone was certain the man had frozen to death. Some, including Mrs. Atchley and Tish, even hoped he had. They had no sympathy for someone who would deliberately put his own wife and children in harm. The search would resume again after the men had rested.

Marie West lived about three miles from the Ramsey shack. She got up early every morning to milk her cow. She dreaded going out on such an icy morning but knew she couldn't put old Bossie off. She expected the milk would freeze in a stream on its way into the pail. Marie trudged through the snow, already frozen into a thick crust. When she walked into the barn, she let out a scream and dropped the bucket as she and the cow bolted from the barn.

The scream woke Ramsey, he had been asleep face down in the hay. He got up and began walking towards his shack. His head was hurting, and he was suddenly aware of the cold. Some of the money from the coal was still in his pocket. When he got to the shack, he opened the door and stepped inside. He saw his wife and two live children but the baby was dead. There was no furniture left, they had burned it. The woman looked at her husband as she picked up the shotgun that leaned in the corner.

"You forgot this, you could have sold it instead of the coal, but, no . . . you never would sell it. You always said a man had to have a gun, no matter what. Well, let me tell you something, Mister," she paused and pointed to the dead infant, then continued, "a family has to have heat, no matter what." She lifted the gun and pulled the trigger. Ramsey was knocked all the way across the room. His body lay in a pool of blood. He died much the same as he had lived, barely conscious of what was going on around him.

The dawn or hunger woke Tish early. Since she had skipped supper last night, it was no wonder she woke up hungry. While the coffee was brewing, she poured some cereal in a bowl. It was the quickest thing she could think of to eat. Collecting her thoughts as she finished her breakfast, she decided to phone Alex to find out about the Ramsey family. She knew he might still be asleep, but she didn't care. She needed to find out about that poor family and the sooner the better.

"Hello, Mary," Alex' wife had answered the phone. "Sorry to call so early, but I wanted to talk to Alex." There was a long pause while Tish waited for Alex to come to the phone.

"Listen, Tish, It's all arranged for us to pick up the children today. There was no way I could do anything last night. The whole town was frozen, shut down. Geez, it still is." Alex prepared himself for the verbal assault he knew was coming. He held the phone away from his ear.

"Damn, Alex, you promised me! I would've gone back out there myself." Tish slammed the phone down. She was too worried to waste time yelling at Alex, maybe someone in the Rescue Squad had taken the family in.

After calling her father to ask him to feed the horses for her, she headed directly out to the shack to see if they were still there. Since she didn't notice any activity in the area, she assumed that Ramsey had been found. As she walked toward the crude building, she noticed the door was half open. Sighing in relief, she assumed the family had been taken someplace. Then, as she turned to leave, she heard the sobbing children. She stepped inside and almost fell over the lifeless body of the man. She felt her stomach tighten as she began to weave.

"I've got to get hold of myself," she told herself. She sat down on the mattress holding the now hysterical children. For some minutes she had trouble focusing her attention on anything, then she saw Mrs. Ramsey sitting on the floor holding her dead infant, the shotgun lay nearby.

"Mrs. Ramsey," Tish whispered.

The woman made no response.

"I'll get help," Tish ran from the shack taking the children with her. She put them in the cab of the truck and squeezed in the driver's seat beside them and drove straight to the Sheriff's office.

The children were placed in foster homes that day. Thankfully, the youngest ones were able to stay together. Mrs Ramsey was taken to jail and charged with shooting her husband. Tish felt sorry for her, but the woman seemed beyond caring what happened to her. Somehow, Tish believed there would be better times ahead for the woman and her surviving children. She didn't see how things could be worse than they had been out there in the stark cold.

Tish went home. She didn't have any liquor in the house except for a couple of bottles of Emmett's moonshine which she had hidden even from herself. She supposed she would keep bumping into one here and there for years to come. She remembered seeing one in the linen closet. Getting it, she drank straight from the bottle. It tasted like something she had never experienced before and had no desire to try again, but it did the job she hoped it would. She stopped shaking from the cold and shock of the day. She also shook from anger. Alex should not have let this happen. A baby would be alive today if he had done what he promised. She had to admit, she did not care much about the man; only the poor woman who had been pushed to the brink of insanity.

She suddenly thought about Marlo. Was this how easily one fell into drinking? She would make a point of trying to talk to Marlo about getting out and doing things. She felt Marlo's largest problem was boredom and that terrible feeling that life was passing her by. It happened to lots of people, especially women who were always conscious of their biological clocks.

She watched the news on the Knoxville station. They showed the old Harlow shack in the film footage as well as the front of the jail where Mrs. Ramsey was being held. She flipped through the channels, trying to find something to take her mind off of the events of the day, but could not stop thinking about little Zeke Ramsey and the sadness in his eyes when she left him with the foster family. Children shouldn't have to bear such misery.

CHAPTER FIVE

"Where have you been," questioned her mother as Tish landed like a guided missile in the big leather chair by the kitchen chimney.

"Riding with Julie," was the faint answer. She prepared herself for the lecture that would surely follow.

"Tish, I know you and Julie have been friends all your life, but now that you're grown, I wish you'd be a little more selective about choosing your friends. Julie has developed a terrible reputation; its bound to rub off on you. There is an old saying about people seeking their own level. You know I liked Julie when she was a child, although she didn't come from our caliber of people. I'm sure poor old Pa and Ma Ferguson did the best they could to rear her, but I'm afraid she's going to end up like her mother. I don't want you painted with that brush.

Can't you spend more time with Marlo and less time with her?" Finally, Rebecca paused for breath, but she wasn't finished.

Tish patiently listened to the same presentation she had heard countless times before. Her mother was probably one of the most generous women in the valley with her love and concern for others, but she had a blind spot when questions of reputation and morality were concerned.

"Mother, please try to understand. Just because Julie is popular with men does not mean that she is wild. She is fun to be around and pretty. They like her. She's had more proposals than anybody I've ever heard of. If she was wild, they wouldn't want to marry her, would they?"

"But her mother ran off with that sorry salesman and just left little Julie." Rebecca said.

"I know, I know. But Julie is not like her mother. She is like a sister and I don't care what people say or think, so you might as well stop worrying about me or her. By the way, we did invite Marlo to go riding with us but she declined."

Rebecca slammed the cake pan she was holding into the oven lapping the batter dangerously close to the pan's rim. "Alright, LaTisha, have it your way, you always do. I guess we spoiled you since you came along so much later than your sisters." she mumbled on but Tish made believe she didn't hear and started getting ready to leave.

Tish walked through the woods toward her cottage. She pulled off her boots so she could feel the soft pine needles against her feet. It was the first warm day of the year. Spring had put up a fierce struggle trying to push aside the cruelest winter the valley could remember.

Julie Percy bounced into her apartment with the gaiety that was part of her. Her place was unique in the valley. Julie's parents were divorced, and she had seen her father only six times since her eighth birthday; she had seen her mother even less. But her grandparents had treated her so well, making her feel so very special that she did not harbor bitterness towards any of them. She had gotten a secretarial job at the County Courthouse shortly after graduation from high school and rented this apartment with her first paycheck. After that, she proceeded to decorate it by dragging whatever was available into it. What she had been unable to paint or varnish, she suspended from the ceiling or nailed to the walls. During a vacation trip to Florida with Marlo, she had been fascinated by the decor of a little fish house. She bought fishnet, collected conk shells and starfish from the beach, searched for driftwood and returned to the valley with her finds which she carefully arranged on one wall of her living room. Next, she spent nearly a week's salary buying an aquarium and tropical fish. She had always been enchanted by plants and had amassed a wilderness of potted greenery. The total effect of the apartment was overwhelming, but somehow it seemed appropriate for her.

If Julie ever suspected that she aroused more than a considerable amount of gossip over the coffee cups of the valley's housewives, she never let it be known. She was openly affectionate, flaunted her sexuality, was seen with a parade of male admirers, and loved life. Julie was not, contrary to popular belief, promiscuous. Her many male friends were kept at bay with such gay and warm refusals, most were filled with hope instead of rejection. Their fascination would bring them back time and time again. Eventually, they learned to cope with the knowledge of the futility of pursuing such a butterfly as Julie. Although she thought of marriage and felt she could become serious about several of the young men she knew, she could not seem to choose just one.

Marlo wondered why she had refused to go riding with Tish and Julie. She hated herself for waiting for the phone to ring. Pacing the dining room from end to end, placing each step neatly into the squares of the rug pattern, she promised herself she would not walk to the decanter and its tempting contents. She was serious about controlling her drinking. The elegant furniture glistened from recent polishing. She wondered why she hoped Alex would call when everything in her protested the sordidness of the whole affair. She left the downstairs to wander to her bedroom where she sat at her dressing table and began brushing her hair. Noticing a few lines around her eyes, she drew closer to the mirror. Her face seemed to taunt her. She had no problem being attractive, but she felt she had already passed her prime. She reviewed her loveless life and wondered where she had gone wrong and deprived herself of the simple goals she had nurtured; just to fall in love, get married and have a family. Marlo never desired anything else. Her fortune had made it unnecessary for her to think about a career and so she had let life happen to her rather than pursuing it. Yes, she had to acknowledge that she had missed opportunities in the past when she had failed to give interested men encouragement. None had intrigued her like Alex did. She smiled as she thought of his handsome features, his strong arms embracing her and thrilling her with his kisses. Why couldn't she have gotten to know him first, before he met Mary and had children. She wanted a drink badly. Suddenly, she rose from the dressing table, picked up her car keys, and drove away from the temptation.

Marlo knocked on Tish's door, she was near panic.

Tish hardly had the door open when Marlo flew by her.

"I wasn't sure you'd be back from your ride. I really wish I had gone."

"I'm glad you came," Tish said, "I haven't seen

much of you lately."

Marlo dropped her eyes and her lips began to quiver. "Tish, I've been stoned all week. I drink every single day. I can't seem to stop myself!"

"Marlo, I think recognizing the problem is a big step to overcoming it." Tish's voice was soft.

"Drinking is the only thing that helps me forget what a silly, lonely life I have. Tish, I've had every advantage and just look at me. I will be thirty soon, and I have nothing to show for my existence. All I ever wanted was someone I could love and a house full of children. Oh, I wish I was dead."

Tish listened as Marlo talked, knowing that the worry she and Julie had felt about their friend was justified.

"Marlo, I have noticed how unhappy you have been lately. I'm glad you have come to talk things over. About your drinking, since you can afford the best clinic in the country, have you considered going to one? You know, they could help you deal with your depression too."

"I don't understand you." Marlo was focused on the own thoughts and did not seem to hear or acknowledge the suggestion Tish had made. "How can you be so happy without someone to love?"

"I suppose most of us hope to find a special person to share our lives with, Marlo, but I don't think we can depend on anyone for our inner peace."

"Are you talking about religion?"

"No, although everyone's spiritual life does matter. I just feel you have blinded yourself to what's around you by concentrating on your dreams. Go to a clinic and get some therapy. But, meanwhile, hang out with me and I'll put you to work!" Tish was trying to be upbeat but she was very concerned about Marlo. Something was different about her. She seemed guilt ridden.

Marlo was quiet for several minutes, then said, "Maybe I'll do just that, but I still don't understand why I haven't been able to find someone to marry; most people do."

"It's probably because of that crust of yours."

"What crust?" Anger flew from Marlo's eyes.

"I don't mean to offend you. It's just that you have so much reserve, it walls you in. No one can get to know you. You give people the impression you aren't interested in anything or anyone."

"Oh, Tish, you know I don't mean to, I've always wished I could be easier with people. I do care. I want them to like me, what can I do to change?"

"I'm not an analyst, Marlo, but I think you should get a volunteer job, since you don't need a paying one. You could help people who need you. I believe if you got involved, you'd just naturally come out of your shell."

"Thanks, Tish, for being straight with me. You have made me feel better, like there is hope. I know I have to stop feeling sorry for myself." They were both quiet again, then Marlo brightened and said, "Do you suppose we'll end up like Dori and Dottie

Freeman?" They both began to laugh.

"We could do worse, they really are a pair." Tish smiled as she thought of the spinster twins. "Come on, let's go visit them. It will give you a chance to see that there is some joy in spinsterhood."

Marlo was hesitant, but anything was better than brooding about herself and Alex so she followed Tish to the car.

"I guess there's not a town in the world that doesn't have its characters and at least one set of spinster sisters." Tish laughed. She loved to visit the Freeman home and did as often as she could. Located at the edge of town, the white frame house was situated on a large lot. Tish parked in the driveway and walked to the house as Marlo followed. Dora opened the door at once.

"Come in, girls! Dottie," she called, "company!" The twins beamed happily as they showed their guests into the parlor. Everywhere were shelves filled with tiny figurines. A large bowl contained artificial fruit mixed with real fruit, Marlo sat in a sagging stuffed chair while Tish shared the sofa with three cats. Marlo never ceased to marvel at the exact likeness of the twins. A crow, perched on top of his cage seemed oblivious to everyone.

"Miss Dotti," Tish asked, "do the cats ever bother Rupert?"

"Oh, mercy, no, but every now and then, he gets wild and scares the daylights out of them." One of the cats jumped in Dottie's ample lap. Dora had disappeared into the kitchen and reappeared carrying a tray filled with cake and coffee.

Marlo and Tish enjoyed the cake that the Freemans were famous for throughout the valley. They were enjoying the chatter of the elderly women when they were startled by a sudden creaking noise on the stairs in the hall. Marlo looked up and turned to Tish.

"Don't be concerned," Miss Dotti said reassuringly, "it's only Papa. Now, as I was saying, Rupert has a bad habit of stealing jewelry, or picking it up and hiding it." Dotti continued talking about the crow but Marlo and Tish were no longer listening. They looked at each other because they knew that Mr. Freeman had been dead for 25 years.

During the drive back to Tish's cottage, Marlo asked, "Have you ever heard Papa before?"

Tish laughed. "I have heard lots of noises in that house, but I am not convinced they were caused by Mr. Freeman's ghost. Have you heard the story about the tombstone?"

"No," Marlo's eyes widened.

"Well, Mr. Freeman was buried in the church cemetery. The family ordered a headstone to mark his grave. For some reason, it was delivered to the house instead of the cemetery. I was told that Dora instructed the men to put it on the porch temporarily. Anyway, there it stayed year after year with them intending to have it moved but never getting around to it. Finally, the wooden floor of the porch began to sag and creak, but they still did not move the stone. It was not until Miss Dora fell through the floor one day and suffered a broken ankle that a carpenter was called to fix the porch. He moved the stone out into the yard. There it stayed for several more years with the family continuing to say they were going to have it moved to the cemetery. Then old Mrs. Freeman died. She left instructions to be buried in the new Woodlawn Memorial Gardens. Naturally, the twins carried out her wishes. It was then that they first reported the presence of their father's ghost. I can remember Miss Dotti saying, 'Poor Papa is upset because we haven't put up his stone. Although he's been very patient with us, he's tired of waiting.' So, at last, the stone was placed at the grave site." Tish paused while she parked the car and she and Marlo entered her cottage. After they were seated, she continued the story, "The ghost of their father continued to disturb them and the poor ladies were beside themselves. I was over there one day helping them pick beans when Miss Dotti came running straight through the garden with beans flying out of her apron. She was shouting, 'I've got it!'"

"'You've got what?' " Miss Dora asked, 'sun on your brain! Look at all those beans you dropped!'"

"'I know what's troubling Papa!' Miss Dotti yelled, 'he is worried and upset because we buried Mama so far from him.' They stood there beaming at each other wondering why they hadn't thought of it before. We left the garden and went to drink lemonade on the porch. After a great deal of discussion, they decided to move the remains of their father since his spirit was the one who stayed up moving around so much."

Marlo laughed hysterically, Tish realized that it had been a very long time since she had heard Marlo laugh and was delighted to see her friend in good humor for a change.

"There's more to the story," Tish said, "if you want to hear it."

"Oh, yes, please!" Marlo responded.

"The day the body was to be moved, they asked me to drive them to the cemetery. I did. After the coffin was lifted from the ground and loaded onto the hearse, Mr. Jones asked the sisters what he should do with the stone. You know, Woodlawn Cemetery does not allow upright headstones, they require all the graves be marked by identical flat markers. Anyway, when Mr. Jones asked the sisters, they just shrugged their shoulders. Then Miss Dotti said, 'Just drop it in the hole; I reckon St. Peter will know where to find him come Judgment Day.'"

"Wonder what they'll do next to try to get rid of his ghost." Marlo asked.

"They have decided now that the ghost hangs around simply because he wants to keep on staying there. They say they have learned to accept his presence."

"Tish, you really have managed to get my mind

off myself. I have laughed more today than I have in months. Do you mind if I stay for supper?"

"Mind? I insist!"

They decided to dine outside on the little patio outside the kitchen to enjoy the seasonal view of the yard and distant fields. Spring was one of the prettiest Marlo could remember. Or, perhaps she had been too inebriated before to notice. The Dogwood trees were loaded with blooms this year, as were the Redbuds. Together, their branches made a canopy for the buttercups and narcissus growing in clumps below them. Tulips, with their vibrant colors seemed to be calling for her attention. She smiled with genuine appreciation of nature's gifts of beauty.

As early blooms began to fade and fall from the trees, the azaleas began to open and shout with their loud, full palate of colors. Spring was reaching its peak too quickly for Tish who wanted it to last as long as possible. The near perfect weather continued, with just the right amount of rainfall and sunshine. People were pleased with their gardens and most were unusually upbeat during the respite from the cold dreary days of winter. Not even the yearly thunderstorms dampened their enthusiasm. Julie and Tish were delighted to see how much progress Marlo was making in her battle with alcohol. She promised them that she would go to a clinic if she could not stay sober, but was determined to try first at home. They spent many afternoons lying in the sunshine by the pool at the estate. It was not yet warm enough to swim, but created a relaxing ambiance for them.

Marlo was doing better giving up alcohol than she was at giving up Alex. She still yearned to be with him. She reasoned with herself that it was natural to have the feelings she had, it was just for the wrong person. She wished she could tell Tish and Marlo, but couldn't bring herself to do so. She guessed it was because of the shame she felt. Also, neither of them liked Alex and probably wouldn't understand why she was so in love with him. It was during these times of brooding that she felt the urge to turn back to her bar for its temporary solace.

Marlo wondered how it was possible for Alex to know when she was at her most vulnerable, for that was when he seemed to drop by. He managed to visit when the servants were gone. His boyish good looks always disarmed her. She both loved and detested his lust for her and she him.

A persistent drizzle had changed all of Tish's plans for the day. Since it was Saturday, she was determined not to think about her job. She tried to find some interest in the projects she always planned to do on some rainy day. She couldn't find a book that she hadn't already read, so she picked up the swatches of material she had saved to make a quilt. It was something she had never done before. Settling herself down with needle, thread and scissors, she cut all the little wedges for one section

and proceeded to sew some of the little sections together to make one square of nine little ones. It was
going to be a nine diamond quilt; that was the design she had chosen. It was supposed to be the
easiest for beginners, according to her Grandmother
Jensen. After she finished the first square, she held
it up in front of her, staring in bewildered impa-
tience. How could anyone piece together and entire
quilt, she wondered as she bundled up the would-
be quilt and tossed it in the direction of a basket,
knowing she would give the swatches to some of
the women out in Crazy Creek. They made beautiful
quilts and sold some of them to shops in Townsend
and Pigeon Forge where they were resold to tourists
for much more money than the merchants paid the
ladies to make them. But, that was business and to
be expected. Everyone was satisfied with the arrangement.

So much for that, she thought, and decided to go
out. She pulled on a poncho and walked out into the
soggy gray day. She went to the barn where there
was always plenty of work that needed doing. The
horses looked cozy and lazy in their well-bedded
stalls. There was something special about being in a
barn on a rainy day; perhaps it was the sound of
rain as it pattered on the tin roof and horses munching on their hay, nickering softly welcoming sounds
when she entered. She petted them all, then swept
the tack room and rearranged some of the saddles
and bridles that had been put away quickly. Sitting

on a box, she soaped her saddle and rubbed it dry with a towel, watching the leather take on a satiny sheen. The billet straps seemed to be a little dry so she applied an ample amount of Leather New. She wondered how Marlo was doing and decided to go see her because she hadn't talked to her in a couple of days. After giving the horses a parting treat, she left the barn.

While she was driving, the sky seemed to be clearing a little. She drove slowly so she could enjoy seeing the watercolor-like sky as it began to change. The blues looked like droplets moving downward, just like watercolors washing down a tilted paper. She recalled her Grandmother telling her that the Lord was painting his sky.

As Tish ran up the steps of Marlo's house, the sky seemed to tire of the drizzle and opened up with a drenching downpour. She didn't take time to knock; just let herself in and was looking down at the water dripping off her poncho when she heard a door close.

"Hi, Marlo," she called out, "it's me, Tish." She noticed two glasses on the coffee table in the room just off the hall and a familiar shirt monogrammed with the initials A.M. Trying to remember where she had seen that shirt, she heard Marlo in another part of the house.

"Just a minute, Tish," Marlo's voice hinted some irritation. Tish was beginning to realize that she was an unwelcome visitor. Marlo entered then wearing just a robe. Although she was attempting to be hospitable, she seemed uneasy. She froze when she saw the shirt on the sofa.

"My uncle must have left his shirt here last night," she explained feebly as she picked it up, folding it quickly. He stopped by to see if I'd heard about Mom and Dad."

Tish nodded, but she knew Marlo's only living uncle would not wear a shirt monogrammed A.M. when his initials were E.S. She watched Marlo pick up the glasses, the ice nearly melted now, and carry them to the sink. She wished she hadn't come. Trying to think of some way to exit gracefully, she said, "Just thought I'd stop by to see if you wanted to go over to Julie's."

"No, not today," Marlo answered. "I really don't feel well. I think what I need is sleep. I was just dozing when you came."

"Oh, I'm so sorry I disturbed you. I wouldn't have just barged in but it is raining buckets." Tish explained. There was a brief silence when Marlo didn't respond.

"Okay, I'll see you later," Tish said as she was leaving. Once inside her car, Tish felt her cheeks flush. She was feeling a little confused realizing that Marlo was keeping something from her. She also knew that Julie wasn't home so she returned to her cottage.

Hours passed before Alex asked Marlo for the time.

"It's one o'clock on the dot."

"Geez, I've got to get home. Mary might have found out there's not a poker game!"

"Alex, we must stop seeing each other. As much as I love you, I know it isn't right. Our time together is wonderful, but after you leave, I feel just rotten. I can't go on like this."

Please, Marlo, let's not talk about it now. I've got to go."

Marlo cried herself to sleep after Alex left. She decided guilt was harder to bear than alcoholism or loneliness. Why, oh why did she let this affair continue! She was so weak.

Alex Morgan rushed home as quickly as possible. Because Tish had come by, he was certainly glad he had taken the time to park his car in one of the garages. Marlo rarely had unannounced visitors so he usually parked in the driveway for a quick encounter. But last night, he knew he was going to be staying for quite sometime, at least the length of an average poker game, however long that might be. A man of many conflicts, he had dreamed in his youth of becoming a bank president or a politician or almost anything that would allow him to look and feel superior to his station in life. He had no illusions of having great intelligence or talent. He knew his was, as his grades reflected, average. He also recognized his love of comfort and lack of drive. He

SARAH SIMPSON BIVENS

did not acknowledge the fact that he was lazy. Because his older brother had managed to gain some influence, Alex was given his job, Supervisor of Human Services. And, due to the unbridled energy of Tish Jamison, his agency had risen to prominence in the State. Tish's evaluations were hard-hitting and impressive. Alex had enjoyed taking the credit and was currently being considered for an appointment with the state administrative office.

He pulled into the driveway of his modern split-level home in one of the town's more desirable neighborhoods. Professionally landscaped, a hedge outlined a neatly clipped lawn. He closed the door quietly and let himself in the house. As he moved down the hall, he was relieved to hear the rhythmic breathing of his sleeping wife. He went into the bathroom and prepared to brush his teeth. Nothing could prevent Alex from this task, for his teeth were his most prized feature. Perfectly formed, an even row of enameled surfaces appeared in the mirror, glistening under his brush. Alex was attractive. He was of medium height, medium complexion, medium sized nose. Just about everything about him was medium, he observed. His hair wasn't straight, wasn't curly. It was styled and fit his head neatly. Pleased at his image, he switched off the light and tiptoed into the bedroom to join his sleeping wife. Lying next to Mary, he thought of Marlo. Before he had begun the affair with Marlo, he had been happy with Mary. She was a good mother, a dutiful wife,

94

and a civic leader. He knew that he was risking his entire image in the community by seeing Marlo. He thought of his small sons asleep in another room. Yet, he knew he would sacrifice his soul for Marlo. She was everything he wanted to be. He would never give her up. Never.

CHAPTER SIX

"I'm sure going to miss you, honey," Margaret said as she helped Marlo pack. "Seems like this would be the worst time of year down there. As hot as it's been here, just think what it'll be like that far south."

"You're right about that," Marlo agreed, "but I'd better go while I'm in the mood. You know how often they call begging me to come."

"Yes, that's right enough. You should spend more time with your folks. I expect they're in their 70's now. You'll regret it when they're gone if you don't. Believe me, I know."

Marlo embraced Margaret at the door before leaving for the airport. "Margaret," she said, "I love you. Will you do me a favor and call Tish and Julie? They'll be upset if I leave town without letting them know." Margaret nodded, then watched as the car disappeared down the long winding drive. Poor child, Margaret thought, poor child. She could sense Marlo's determination was clouded by depression, but about what, she could not fathom.

Marlo enjoyed the flight to Clearwater, Florida. She was relieved to have distance between Alex and herself. She was not just running away from her problems, she told herself, because it had been a long time since she had visited her parents. They had been thrilled when she had phoned them.

Gloria and Ralph Scott had arrived at the airport early, anxious to see their daughter. They had not seen her since their annual Christmas visit to Jensen's Valley. They could not understand why she preferred to live in a place so devoid of social activity. Both were dressed in cool white slacks and lightweight knit tops with nautical trim showing off their youthful appearance which belied their years. They did love their boat and their friends who also owned boats, or more specifically, yachts. They stood eagerly watching as the plane landed and passengers began leaving the plane.

"There she is!" Gloria yelled as Marlo descended the ramp.

Marlo rushed to her parents encircling both in her arms. After initial greetings were exchanged, Marlo said, "You both look younger, not older. I do believe this climate agrees with you."

"You are browner than we are," Ralph commented, "noticing his daughter's tan. Guess you've been swimming in the pool."

"Sure have." Marlo smiled. "Tish and Julie have been over a lot and that's what we do, lounge around the pool."

On the drive to the gated waterfront community where the Scotts had a four bedroom condominium overlooking the gulf, Marlo enjoyed the scenery, the palm trees which lined the highway were interspersed with palmetto plants. So different than back home, she thought. Noticing how vast and blue the sky looked, she wondered if maybe this was where she should stay. She wasn't sure what it was that kept her in Jensen's Valley since she had been miserable there in recent years. After she was settled in her room, she would go for a nice swim in the gulf. She had to stay, at least long enough to be rid of Alex.

During the first few days, the Scotts noticed the change in their daughter's personality. Instead of the little-girl sadness they had come to expect in her eyes, there was mature laughter. Instead of forbidding reserve in her manner, there was now enthusiasm. Through the years, all the efforts they had mustered to give joy to their daughter had failed. Now, they thought, something has changed. She seemed to have found herself.

"Marlo, dear, are you in love?"

"No, why?" Marlo was shocked at her mother's perception.

"Well, I thought . . . you just seem so much happier."

"I did have a big crush on someone who seemed to like me a lot, but we were wrong for each other. I thought it might be easier to get over him off the mountain, out of the valley, if you know what I mean." Marlo blurted out the truth.

"Who?"

"I'd rather not go into that. It's over and I don't want to talk about it."

"Alright, dear, We're just thrilled to have you with us, whatever the reason."

"Although I'm suffering a little, I feel much better about myself now. I have been feeling useful. I am giving piano lessons to some kids that Tish has rounded up. I'm not charging them anything; they're kids who couldn't afford to take lessons from the other piano teachers, but they're very talented."

"That's wonderful, Marlo, I'm so proud of you." Gloria gave her daughter a hug.

"And, I've learned that I am capable of being loved." Marlo added.

"Well, of course you are dear. You've always known that, haven't you?"

"No, Mother, I didn't know."

Gloria didn't understand, but she decided she wouldn't probe any deeper. She would simply be grateful for the change.

Marlo had been with her parents for almost a week before they announced that they were giving a little beach party in honor of her visit. Marlo smiled, remembering how she had once dreaded such affairs, always resenting the pressure of meeting new people. The harder she had tried to make light-hearted small-talk, the more frozen her tongue had become. Now she discovered, she was looking forward to meeting new people. She was also pleased at how seldom she thought of Alex. There were still some restless nights when she dreamed of their being together. Give it time, she thought.

When Joseph Hathworth was summoned by the Scotts to attend a party for the purpose of meeting their daughter, he was filled with dread. Such invitations were usually for purposes of match-making. He had never yet met an appealing daughter of a rich family. Most of them were either ugly or burdened by arrogant personalities both of which he would prefer to avoid. Yet, there was no way he could decline the invitation since he planned to enter the race for a U.S. Congressional seat. Not wishing to offend his most affluent supporters, he would be forced to grin and bear the ordeal. Besides, he suddenly remembered, he had heard the Scott's daughter was a real beauty which probably meant she would be an insufferable bore.

When Joseph walked onto the softly lighted patio, he was not at all prepared for the beautiful young woman who greeted him. How could he possibly be nice to the daughter, he wondered, when there was someone so alluring as the golden beauty who had just taken his hand to lead him out among the other guests.

"I'm Marlo Scott," she said, "You must be Joseph. My parents told me how handsome you were."

Joseph could hardly believe his ears. These were not the words of a snob. "Marlo?" he asked, his surprise becoming obvious.

"Yes," she said, "what did you expect?" Marlo's eyes were teasing.

Joseph found himself laughing and confessing to his preconceived notion. He was enchanted. He could not understand how such a striking young woman could have escaped the snare of a man for this long. Marlo, too, could not still the feelings that were stirring in her. She had not experienced this kind of excitement since Alex. And, according to her parents, there was more to Joseph than his good looks. She studied the dark hair, the square line of his jaw. There was something elegant about the way he carried his lean towering frame, making him appear even taller than he was. She tried to fathom the wistful look in his eyes.

The party was just the beginning which evolved into glorious days and nights. They swam in the warm salty gulf, letting the tide carry their bodies. Moonlight picked up the droplets of water that rushed over them and dotted her hair like sequins. Joseph felt something catch in his throat as he watched her. Neither appeared to notice the effect they had on the other.

SARAH SIMPSON BIVENS

The days seemed to merge as they spent most of their time together. They tried new restaurants, discovered little out-of-the-way beach clubs and danced to small combos and walked the shorelines quietly happy being together. Neither of them could say exactly when they knew they were in love. Marlo's parents were delighted. It thrilled them to see their daughter in such a happy trance. It was even more perfect because, in a practical way, the match was ideal. Marlo would be the perfect wife for a member of Congress and he the proper husband for the daughter of an influential family.

They decided they would all travel to Jensen's Valley to give Joseph an opportunity to see the place where Marlo grew up and called home. It would be a pleasant way to escape the heat of the Florida sun. They planned the trip around Joseph's busy schedule of political meetings.

Gloria and Ralph relaxed after dinner. "It doesn't seem right that we have to stay indoors to keep cool," Gloria said.

"Well, it won't be long before we will be in Tennessee. We can sit outside and enjoy the evening breezes the way we used to before there was such a thing as air-conditioning." Ralph said.

"Wonder when Marlo will get in tonight?"

"Pretty early, I imagine, Joseph has a busy day tomorrow." Gloria sighed happily. "Should we have the wedding down here or in the valley?"

"There hasn't been anything said about marriage

yet, Gloria, they are not engaged!" Ralph looked at his wife, "You'd best not get your hopes up too high."

"Oh, Ralph, it's just a matter of time. Just look at the way they look at each other. Have you ever seen two people so much in love?"

"We were," he said, winking at his wife, remembering.

"Aren't we still?" they shared a single sigh.

CHAPTER SEVEN

Tish looked at Alex as he sat at a desk across the room from her. For some reason, he was not in his private office. She finished making a list of the home visits she planned for the day. Although she spent as little time as possible in the office, necessity prevented her from staying away altogether. She came in often enough to notice how miserable he looked. She didn't know very much about his personal life so she had no idea what might be bothering him. She wished only that he would resolve whatever it was that was causing him to behave in the bullying manner he had come to prefer. She watched silently as he abruptly left the room.

"He's been a real jackass lately, hasn't he Mabel?" Tish whispered to the secretary.

"He sure has. At least you've got a reason to get

out of here. I have to stay here all day." Mabel pouted.

Alex didn't care what time of day it was, he was going to drive by the Scott estate to see if there was any sign of Marlo. He was going crazy, he thought, if he tried to concentrate on his work, he kept seeing Marlo flaunt herself in his mind's eye. He would see to it that she never left him again. He would make her agree to marry him. Then, he would ask Mary for a divorce. Dreading the thought of the scandal it would cause, he shuddered. Marlo would be worth it, besides, he decided, she had enough prestige to carry them through. No one could blame him for falling victim to someone like Marlo. He would emerge as a hero, who could look down on the man who captured the heart of someone like Marlo? Alex knew the only reason Marlo had left was because he was a married man. He was certain she would want to continue their relationship when he told her he was going to get a divorce. If only it weren't for her parents, he would go to her in Florida. Perhaps he could phone her. It would be easy enough to get the number from Tish or Margaret. He couldn't think of a good enough reason to give them for wanting the number. He'd think of something. There was no sign of life at the Scott estate. Disappointed, Alex drove back to the office.

"Guess what, Alex," Tish said brightly, "I got a card from Marlo."

Alex tried to still the sudden jumping of his

heart. Attempting to be casual, he asked, "What news did she send?"

"Not much, just that she and her parents will be coming home soon and that she will have a surprise for me."

"Oh," Alex said, hope surged through him. He didn't know how he would manage to see her with her parents in the house, but he would see her somehow. After he told her about his plans for a divorce, she would agree to meet him. Mabel and Tish were relieved to see that Alex started behaving more like his old self, always a jackass, but a tolerable one now.

Tish didn't know exactly when Marlo would return to the valley. She hated to be gone when Marlo brought the surprise she had promised, but she had promised to visit her sisters. Jennifer was living in Atlanta and Susan in Memphis. They came home to visit often but she had never been to see them in their homes. And, she needed to take some vacation days. She couldn't visit one without hurting the feelings of the other, so she had planned double visits on one trip. It was surprising how much they had become like their mother, she wondered if she had also. Tish found the trip enjoyable and interesting. She surveyed the flat land along the Mississippi and decided that Memphis was a very lively place with musicians playing and singing the blues on Beale Street, the lids of their instrument cases open for tips. She also found Atlanta to be quite exciting, a real change of pace, especially when it came to shopping. Her sister kept telling her she just had to go in one more store to see what all they had on display. Tish bought more clothes than she ever had at one time although she wondered where in the world she would wear some of them. Although she was having a much better time than she had expected, neither city could ever take the place of the natural, uncluttered beauty of the Valley and mountains she called home.

She found, much to her surprise, that she really enjoyed being with her sisters. It was a shame, she thought, that they had been so bossy and offensive when they were growing up. She also liked both of their husbands who aided the efforts of her sisters in showing her a good time. All in all, Tish thought, the trip went well. She returned to the valley feeling refreshed by the change, although, she acknowledged, it was good to be back where she belonged.

Tish met Julie for doughnuts and coffee at the Downtown Cafe to catch up on news in the valley and to give a summary of her trip. She learned from Julie that Marlo had not yet returned. Tish was delighted that she would be around to greet her friend at her homecoming. It didn't take much effort to get back into the working routine. She was pleased to learn that Jason Webb had passed his equivalency tests and was preparing to enter the University of Tennessee. Not bad, she thought, for someone who had dropped out of school so young.

Tish had circled September 8 on her desk calendar. It was a day she had anticipated with both pleasure and dread. She was to drive to the State Prison for Women to pick up Molly Ramsey who was to be paroled that day for the shotgun slaying of her husband. She was to take the Ramsey children from their foster homes to be reunited with their mother in an apartment that had been acquired for them. According to prison officials, Mrs. Ramsey had been a model prisoner who seemed to be transformed from the therapy she was able to get while there. They were convinced she could adequately fill her role as mother to her three children with aid provided by the State. The apartment secured through the Department of Human Services was within walking distance of town. A trainee position has been arranged for her in the kitchen of the valley's best restaurant. Molly Ramsey, who had never had much of a chance in life, would now have a new beginning.

Tish had never been to a prison before. When the great walls came into view, she felt threatened. At the gate, she was informed that her charge would be brought out. She was both relieved and disappointed that she would not see inside the prison walls. Waiting, she sat on a bench near the gate. Minutes later, she watched a plump young woman wearing a cotton dress, accompanied by a uniformed guard, walk towards the gate. Molly came near enough to Tish to finally be recognized. Under different circumstances, Tish doubted that she would have known this healthy looking young woman to be the same frail person she had seen on that cold winter morning. Molly's cheeks bloomed; she looked her age, for a change, instead of the aging old woman of the past.

Settled with Molly in the car for the long ride back to Jensen's Valley, Tish tried to start a conversation. "I'll bet you have looked forward to this day."

"No," Molly stared through the windshield, avoiding Tish's eyes.

"I don't understand," Tish said with genuine disbelief. "You haven't seen your children since . . ." she did not know how to complete the sentence.

"Oh, I do want to see the kids," she paused, "it's just that I'm afraid."

"What are you afraid of Mrs. Ramsey?"

"Call me Molly, please," for the first time since they left the prison, there was a smile on her lips, then it was gone. "The prison is the only place I was ever wanted, really. They were nice to me. I didn't like some of the other prisoners, but I was able to keep to myself mostly. And some of the guards were hateful, kind of throwing their weight around, but most of them were alright. They put me to work in the kitchen." Smiling again, she continued, "You have never seen so much food in your life. Fixing meals is real nice when you've got everything you need. I learned a lot of new things to make, things I hadn't ever eaten before. And, Miss Jamison . . ."

"If you want me to call you Molly," Tish interrupted her, "you have to call me Tish."

"All right, Tish," Molly said, "I was fixing to tell you how warm the prison was. I wasn't cold, not once, not even in the middle of winter. And the letters the foster people have been sending me about my kids; well, I know they been getting along just fine. I'm just afraid we might get back in the same shape we were in before. I might could stand it for myself, but I just couldn't stand to ever see my kids go hungry and cold again."

"Molly," Tish began, intently, "It'll never happen again if you don't take up with the likes of that husband you had. Just don't even give a man like that the time of day. The Prison told us what a hard worker you are and a good cook. You'll do just fine in the job we've got waiting for you, and you're going to like the apartment. I can't wait for you to see it."

"But, Tish, what if the kids don't want me for a mother anymore . . .after what I did to their pa?" Molly's lip began to quiver.

"They understand, really, they do. We explained to them how terribly upset you were after your little baby died. They know, too, what their pa did. They understand enough, believe me. They can't wait for you to get back to them."

Molly remained doubtful and the conversation lapsed into silence. It was not until Tish witnessed the reunion of mother and children in their new home that her own anxiety lessened. She watched Zeke hug away all the fear and apprehension from his mother's drawn features. Somehow, the bloody image of the corpse of Clyde Ramsey faded into the past leaving a kindling hope for the future.

Tish filled the bathtub and eased her tired body into it. Lazily, she bathed, dreading the effort of removing herself from the tub. As she dried herself, she imagined Molly in her new home, everything new and clean. The three children looked so happy, she almost choked holding back her tears.

The following day at the office, Tish received another card from Marlo and noticed it was addressed to her home. Tish wondered how it had gotten in the office mail. That was one thing about the valley postal service, she thought, they didn't pay much attention to addresses as long as they knew the intended recipient. The card said there had been a slight delay, but she would be returning shortly.

Tish didn't know that Alex had already read the card. He had, in fact, made a point of checking the mail each day to see if there was any news from Florida. His patience was running thin and his mood swings were evident to everyone. If Marlo didn't return soon, he was not at all sure what would happen to him. There was not a night spent without dreams of her. He found himself staring at his wife bitterly, wishing she would vanish before his eyes. Mary had noticed his behavior. Since Alex was too young for a typical mid-life crisis, she assumed the pressures of his job were stressing him. He had always been difficult. It was hard to remember a time when he was happy or even content. Lately, even the children questioned her about Alex's lack of interest.

Alex considered going ahead and telling Mary he wanted a divorce. But, where would he go? No, he had to wait on Marlo. They would figure it out together. He knew he couldn't move in with her until after they were married. They'd have to rent a hide-a-way somewhere until they could be married.

CHAPTER EIGHT

Bubbling with laughter, Julie and Tish raced Zeger and Ginger up the Meadow Road. Cutting through the familiar lane that took them into the vast open fields of the Jones farm, Tish noticed clean fence rows instead of the familiar jungled ones. The entire place had a different look about it. Suddenly, she remembered that the deserted place had been sold. Reining her horse to a halt, she waited for Julie to catch up.

"Do you know who bought this place?" Tish asked

"No," Julie shook her head.

"Wonder if we can still ride here?"

A shout descended from the rise above them answering the question intended for Julie.

"Get the hell out of here with those horses! Can't you see I've planted this field!" The voice was very angry.

As Julie and Tish turned their horses, the shouting figure strode down the slope to meet them. As the riders and the man met, Tish and Julie began apologizing at once, not daring to look directly at the forceful figure before them.

"We're sorry," they said in unison, "we've been riding here for years. The farm hadn't been worked since Mr. Jones died six years ago. We just weren't paying any attention. Now, of course, we know. We didn't notice any difference by just looking." Tish glanced hesitantly from the withers of her horse to look at the man.

"The seed has been drilled into the ground. It doesn't disturb the soil like plowing. Look and you can tell."

"Yes, I see," both girls said at once. Then Tish kicked her horse and galloped from the field.

Trying to hold Zeger who was determined to follow Ginger, Julie said, "We are sorry, truly. I'm Julie Percy and that's Tish Jamison," she pointed to the departing rider. "What's your name?"

"Neil Darren."

Julie could no longer control the prancing horse, waving, she allowed Zeger to gallop after Ginger and Tish.

When she caught up with horse and rider, Julie rolled her eyes and said, "Did you get a good look at him?"

"It was hard not to," snapped Tish, "he was

standing right in front of us."

"Yes, but, I mean, did you see beyond the dirt on his clothes? Wow, Tish, he's the best looking thing I've seen in a long time. His name is Neil Darren."

"Have you ever seen a man you did not inspect?" Tish asked sarcastically.

"No," Julie smiled to herself.

Tish reviewed the man in her mind. Tall, lean, he had looked at her with cool blue eyes . . . no, they were cold, she thought. His body had the look of one who works long and hard. She didn't care how handsome he was; he was rude and insensitive.

As he walked back up the slope, Neil muttered to himself, "Tish Jamison . . .Tish . . .," odd name, he thought. There was something about her, he wasn't sure what, only that her eyes had spit fire at him like a hickory log. Horses with that look were a challenge to him, perhaps that was it. And her flying walnut hair reminded him something of a wild horse, not yet tamed. But, now, there was work to do. Climbing back onto the tractor, he looked at the landscape around him. The dark soil flaunted its virility as the machinery bit into it. Neil's hardened features grew slack as he whistled, not hearing the tune drowned out by the loud hum of the engine.

Julie and Tish finished their ride quietly, each one lost in her own thoughts. The ride had been exhilarating. They parted at the forks of Meadow Road, waving goodbyes. Tish allowed Ginger to return home slowly, letting the horse begin to cool.

She wondered how many times she and Julie had said goodbye at the forks of the road. Probably thousands, she thought, since they had been riding together all their lives. Leading Ginger into the barn, she gave her a loving caress as she brushed the lustrous tawny coat. Letting her out in the pasture, Tish watched the mare roll in the grass.

It was only three days later that Marlo, her parents, and Joseph boarded a plane for the flight to Jensen's Valley. No one on board could miss the blossoming love between the attractive young couple. They had been in flight for sometime when Joseph turned his head to the blonde one nestled against his shoulder.

"Do you know what state you are in?" he asked.

"No," she answered.

"Good." he said, "you won't know what state you became engaged in."

Marlo's eyes fluttered open as she felt the ring being slipped on her finger. The size of the diamond was big enough to impress even a rich girl.

"Oh, Joe, she gasped, turning to kiss him, oblivious to the smiling passengers around them Marlo looked at him teasingly, "Why did you want to get engaged up in the air surrounded by all these people?"

"Well, I've been up in the air ever since I met you and how could you say no in front of an audience." She hugged him in spite of the fact that she had fantasized a proposal in a more romantic setting.

Joseph laughed. Marlo casually reached her hand over the back of the seat and dangled it in front of her parents who were sitting behind them.

"Oh!" was the loud shriek from her mother. Just as she and Ralph were lifting themselves from their seats to congratulate the newly engaged couple, they were halted by the flashing sign accompanied by a barking voice over the speaker: "Fasten your seat belts." They were preparing to land.

As the Scotts descended from the plane, they were faced by local reporters who always gave them celebrity status. No one knew how the locals knew when they would be flying in, but somehow, they were always there, cameras flashing. Since Joseph was a heavy favorite in his congressional race, his whereabouts was also well monitored. Not many hours would pass before photographs of the engaged couple would appear in all the area newspapers and in Florida as well.

"I can see why they want to take pictures of Joseph," said Mrs. Scott, "but I can't imagine why they want pictures of us, Ralph. We have no significance whatsoever, except our money."

"One thing I'll say about Clearwater," she continued, "they have so many millionaires they hardly notice us."

Ralph smiled, enjoying the attention. At such times he always felt sad that he was the last male heir to the Scott fortune. Now, though, he turned to

Marlo and Joseph and felt that, although the name would not go on, at least, there was the hope of descendants.

Everyone in Jensen's Valley was buzzing with the news of Marlo's engagement. Alex would have heard the news as quickly as anyone else if circumstances hadn't taken him out of town the day before. He had resented having to leave, but there was no escape from the trip. Mary's mother had been killed in an automobile accident in Chicago where she had been living with her son. Alex had to take his family to the funeral. He was dismayed when he learned that her body wouldn't be returned to the valley for burial. If only he could have feigned illness, he would have sent Mary and the boys without him. He didn't know how long the ordeal would last, considering the peculiarities of his in-laws who believed in long wakes. Trying to console himself, he thought the trip might help pass the tormenting waiting for Marlo's return.

Life filled the Scott estate with endless activity, giving a new glow to the stately old mansion. There were parties arranged to announce the engagement, parties to entertain old friends, parties to acquaint political leaders, and parties for fun. The Scotts dearly loved entertaining and found that guests were eager to fly in from other places to join them. Jostling through them all was Margaret, regal in her role. Tish and Julie were continually being summoned to the estate and quickly became involved in helping with the wedding plans. Marlo and Joseph decided to set the date sometime in late November, after the election. Win or lose, they decided it would be best to avoid the pre-election turmoil since the wedding itself was going to be hectic enough. Tish and Julie were ecstatic about the joy of their friend. They chided Marlo about hitting the jackpot when she met Joseph. Both of them liked him instantly. He returned their admiration telling Marlo how lucky she was to have such good friends.

Joseph had Marlo show him Jensen's Valley and, of course, Crazy Creek. He marveled at the beauty of it, the low-lying gentle fields cradled by the foothills and mountains. Although he had traveled extensively, he was sure he had never seen a place quite like it. The time spun away and it was soon time for him to return to the political whirlwind he had left behind.

"If I don't get back to Florida, the state will disown me. I can't expect Floridians to vote for me if I spend all my time in Tennessee," he told a protesting Marlo.

"I do understand, really," she said, "it's just that I'll miss you so much."

"Why don't you come back with us. You know your parents are going to help me campaign. You could too."

"I will, just as soon as I finalize all the wedding plans. I want to take care of everything before I leave the valley so I can really concentrate on helping you win votes." She turned to face him, "It will take only a couple of weeks here, then I'll be on the first plane south." Going to stand before the massive bay window, she gazed into the horizon. "Oh, Joe, I'm so happy."

Walking to stand behind her, Joseph circled her waist with his arms. "Marlo," he spoke with his lips in her hair, "I cannot believe my own good fortune in finding you."

"I'm glad you're leaving before the Mountain Ride," she said, "it will cushion the blow of saying goodbye."

"You mean you won't miss me while you're on the mountain," he protested.

"No, silly," she scoffed, "but the mountain soothes the lonely heart. Doesn't that sound romantic?"

He turned her to face him, finding her more beautiful each time he looked at her. They kissed and became lost in the moment.

CHAPTER NINE

It was four-fifteen on the lighted dial of the clock radio in the dark bedroom. Tish doubted she had slept more than a couple of hours in the brief snatches of slumber that had marked her night. Apparently she would never outgrow her child-like anticipation of the annual mountain ride. She threw back the covers and got up to wait until it was time to go join the other riders who would gather at Ferguson's stables shortly before dawn. She sat and watched the activity of the coffee maker. The appealing aroma promised vitality. Sipping the coffee, she sank back in her favorite chair enjoying the stillness of the morning. October first, she thought, was better than Christmas. How many years had it been since her first ride? She couldn't remember. Julie's pa had taken the little girls along when they were still quite young. She recalled begging her hesitant parents into letting her go. In all the years since, neither of them had missed a single ride. During the college years, it had not always been easy to get away from campus, but she had managed. Many times Tish had tried to explain the joy of the Mountain Ride, but realized by the doubt in the eyes of non-riders that only a horse lover could fully understand. Another cup of coffee, and it would be time to dress. Gulping down the hot coffee, she felt its warmth spread through her body. She went to the chair to reach for the clothes she had placed there; jeans, tee-shirt, long sleeved shirt, heavy socks and boots. After dressing, she checked the contents of her saddle bags. They contained a poncho, insect repellent, chap stick, hoof pick, ointment, a sponge, a few strands of binder twine and a billet strap; the last two items were for emergency repair of broken tack. Tish added soap, towel, basic toiletries, and a box of raisins. Next, she placed a change of clothing in her bedroll and rolled it up. And finally, she filled the canteen with water and strapped it to her belt. Slinging the saddlebags over her shoulder, she picked up the bedroll and hurried to the car. Ginger had been taken the day before to await the ride in Pa Ferguson's barn where the ride would begin.

As she turned on the lane that headed to the stables, Tish noticed others had arrived before her. Everyone was moving briskly in preparation for the departure. There would be plenty of time later for talking. Ginger was still munching on her morning hay when Tish entered her stall. The mare paused long enough to whinny a greeting. Tish brushed her and carefully saddled her using two saddle blankets. "A hundred miles is a long way, girl, and I don't want you to get any saddle sores." Tish always talked to her horses who seemed to appreciate the reassuring tones even if they did not always comprehend what they were being told. As everyone prepared their mounts, Tish could hear Pa whistling.

Pa Ferguson looked forward to the ride as much as anyone even though most of the work fell his way. As he zipped about the barn, more than one person noted that he never seemed to age. "Five minutes," Pa announced. The riders would leave at 6 o'clock sharp. Pa waited for no one. The riders who occasionally overslept had to catch up the best way they knew how.

Leading Ginger from the barn, Tish saw Julie already mounted. Her long raven hair hung in a single braid.

"Morning," Tish said brightly.

"Morning, yourself," Julie flashed her winning smile. "Have you noticed the new rider?"

"No, I've been busy . . . haven't had time to look around." Swinging into the saddle, Tish saw him, Neil Darren.

Julie enjoyed the frozen expression in Tish's eyes. Having witnessed the tension of their first meeting, Julie wondered what would come of a new encounter between her friend and the newcomer.

"I didn't know he had a horse," Tish said in surprise." What rotten luck that he does."

"It's not his, it's one of Pa's, a new one, in fact. Pa asked Neil if he would ride it to help break it in."

Tish watched as Neil's horse fidgeted nervously. It was a big horse, at least 16 hands high. Tish wondered how Pa knew he could ride.

"Pa knows Neil's parents. They live in Middle Tennessee. He's traded horses with them for years. He says Neil used to start all their colts." Julie spoke admiringly.

Tish was surprised that Pa could be friendly with anyone as rude as Neil Darren. He sure didn't act like he cared for horses when he chased them off his land.

Attempting to change the subject, she asked, "Is Marlo coming?"

"Yes. Joseph and her parents left last night. She is going to the half way point, then she has to come back to select the material for her wedding dress. Did you know she's having it made by some designer in New York? Imagine that." Julie spoke excitedly.

"Speaking of the bride-to-be," Tish turned as she saw Marlo leading Sassy towards them, "and she appears."

Marlo was barely mounted when Pa yelled, "We're off!" The group headed down the lane. It was quite a mixed conglomeration of horse flesh,

Tish observed. There were horses of almost every size and breed. The Tennessee Walkers and other gaited horses ambled along smoothly while the Quarter horses, Appaloosas and a Arabians jogged. There were also a few mules, a Thoroughbred and a number of crosses. A couple of riders had nudged their horses into a slow canter. Regardless of the gaits, the group moved at one speed from the lane across Meadow Road and up the slope which led to the distant silhouette of dense forest. When they arrived at the edge of the woodland, the group broke into a line and entered single file to ride the narrow path. Although the moon provided ample light in the field, foliage darkened the path. The horses moved slowly now, Pa in the lead with his big Buckskin. After about two miles, the path entered an old logging road which permitted the riders to merge into pairs. Tish sensed rather than saw Neil and the dark bay beside her. Her throat became dry with the tenseness she felt. Angry that anyone could distract her in such a way, she stared straight in front of her.

"It's a fine morning, isn't it?" his voice lacked the biting edge of their previous encounter.

"Yes," Tish said flatly, then said defiantly, "Have you had to chase anymore riders out of your fields?"

Neil chuckled, "If you hadn't been in such a hurry, I would have told you what fields I have that were alright to ride in."

125

Tish rode on in silence. She had never been tongue tied in her life, but now, in the black forest beside this bothersome stranger, she was speechless.

Neil did not seem to mind the silence as he watched Tish brushed by the shadows. He noticed how easily she rode, her horse and her body moving as one. He again associated her wild, flying hair, fanning out from her face, with the mane of a mustang. Her straight nose and the defiant set of her mouth were so opposed to his friendliness, he thought, he had best be cautious. Even the oversized flannel shirt could not camouflage the curves of her small body. They rode for several miles in silence. The road widened and led to a clearing where a fire burned brightly. Two stable boys were busy preparing breakfast. Having tied the horses to picket lines, the riders converged around the fire to feast on sausage, biscuits, scrambled eggs and fried apples.

Laughter rang through the still forest as the riders scattered through the clearing carrying plates of food. Tish, Marlo, and Julie sat down at the base of a large tree and ate ravenously. Even Marlo cast her manners aside and ate like a hungry field hand. Tish allowed her eyes to wander about the clearing until she saw Neil seated next to Pa. They were talking with the blacksmith who came on the ride for pleasure but always managed to pick up a little work along the way. Tish turned her attention to her friends just as Julie stretched her hand to display the diamond sparkling on it.

"Marlo, it's all your fault," Julie giggled. "I always told you two that I planned to be the first to reach the altar. Since you went and got yourself engaged, I decided I couldn't put it off any longer."

Tish watched as her friends hugged each other. She too joined in the congratulations. "Who, when?" With Julie, one could not be sure for she dated several men steadily.

"I'm going to marry Jimmy Smith," she said, "sometime before Marlo's wedding." She laughed.

Marlo and Tish nodded approvingly. Jimmy had been a life long boyfriend of Julie's. Others had come and gone, but Jimmy had always been there. He owned a backhoe and a dozer and found his services very much in demand in the area.

"I've loved Jimmy for a long time," Julie whispered, "but I had to be sure. I just wasn't sure I'd be happy tied to anyone. You know what happened to my mother, getting the wanderlust, the grass always greener on the other side, so to speak. I just had to be sure I wouldn't turn out like her."

Tish and Marlo nodded.

"I can remember the first time Jimmy hit on me," Julie said, smiling. "It was in Mrs. Baker's first grade. We had just come in from recess when Jimmy, who sat behind me, put a lizard down the back of my dress."

The laughter from the trio at the large sycamore tree drew the attention of others in the camp.

"It sure did take you a long time to make up your mind about Jimmy if it started in the first grade . . . I mean your love affair." Marlo giggled.

"Will you tell your parents?" Tish asked, serious now.

"No, not unless they phone or come for a visit. I don't care for myself, but I hate to see Ma and Pa so worried."

"I think it is unforgivable that both my best friends plan to desert me at the same time," Tish whimpered, trying to lighten the conversation again.

"Well, you know what they say about major events, like marriage, births and deaths; they happen in threes. You better watch out, Tish Jamison, and pick a good one because you're bound to be next!"

After the breakfast break, the riders mounted their rested horses and continued on the trail. Lunch would be whatever they packed in their saddle bags. Usually, only two meals were prepared on each day of the ride, but Pa sometimes varied his plan, depending on the weather and influences not known to the riders. Sometimes he just liked to surprise them.

As the day advanced, conversation became less animated as the horses and riders began to tire. They stopped for the night at a familiar campsite always chosen for the first night on the trail. Here, once again, Pa's helpers had begun preparations for the evening meal. They already had a campfire glowing when the riders drifted in a few at a time to settle for the night. The meal was less hearty than the send-off breakfast but adequate.

Gradually, riders checked on their horses who were fed and watered earlier in the evening and securely tied on the pickets for the night. Some of them laid down, others began to sleep standing, with one hind foot cocked and ready to strike a would be predator. It was an instinctive gesture that all horses seemed to share if not all at one time. Then the riders prepared for sleep, some in portable tents, others simply in bedrolls spread on the softest spots available.

Dawn came bringing a splendid palette of color to the night sky, cool hues of yellow, lavender, and gray beginning to tint the darkness, then gradually giving way to rosy tones of orange and glints of red as the sun poked its nose above the horizon showing its brilliant yellow light.

The shroud of vibrant light exposed the distance between them and the mountains to which they would ride. Magically, the the full light of morning was on them. Members of the group became self-consciously aware of themselves and their surroundings. Busily they broke camp, picking up debris, washing dishes in the creek, watering and feeding horses, and making ready for the long ride before the lunch stop. Finally, horses were saddled and the riders mounted.

Tish, seated comfortably in her saddle, followed her friends on the trail. She let her senses savor all that was about her, the churning of the little river just below the falls, the glistening of the dew on the foliage, the soft footfalls of the horses on the leaves, and the smell of leather and horses. For some reason, she was never more alert than here on the mountain. The hours passed quickly. Pausing in the middle of a creek, she let Ginger drink her fill, then wading deeper, until the stirrups touched the water, she took the sponge from the saddle bag and dipped it into the cold water. Ginger stretched her neck, enjoying the cooling treat as Tish sponged the sweat from her neck and withers. Marlo joined her with Zeger. Her face was troubled.

"Tish, may I talk with you?" she asked.

"When did you have to ask?" Tish chuckled.

"Tish, I need some advice, I have something . . . uh . . . in my past that I'm not sure I should tell Joseph."

"What is it," Tish asked, thinking she knew everything in her friend's past.

"Do you remember when I was drinking so much? Well, I know that wasn't any excuse for what I did, but . . ." she faltered.

"Go on, Marlo, it can't be all that bad."

"I got involved with a . . . a married man," the words came out in a rush.

Tish was silent for a long time. Finally she said , "Marlo, from what I've seen of Joseph, he is so much in love with you, he'd understand anything, but he might prefer not to know. I can't tell you whether or not you should tell him. Has he told you everything about his past?"

"Not about women, if that's what you mean," Marlo said.

"Then, maybe he doesn't consider the past important. It really is the present that counts."

"It's just that he thinks I'm so damn perfect . . . and I'm not. I want him to know exactly what kind of person he is going to marry . . . how vulnerable I've been . . . the drinking, everything."

"It sounds like you've already made up your mind what you're going to do."

"Not completely, I figured it would be easier to think up here in the mountains."

"I know what you mean," Tish agreed.

They continued across the mountain until they rounded a curve in the trail. Their nostrils picked up the faintest but unmistakable aroma of fish. As they moved closer, the smell was stronger.

"Fried trout!" Tish exclaimed.

"Hush puppies," Marlo echoed, "slaw, potatoes." They were both hungry and knew their horses were ready for a long rest.

"And homemade peach ice cream . . . maybe!" Tish said hopefully.

"There come the stragglers!" someone shouted as Zeger and Ginger poked their heads into view. Since the lunch site was accessible by a road, a big meal was a certainty. Today,the evening meal, higher in the mountains and accessible only by horses, would be less bountiful. Marlo and Tish were the last riders to enter the noon camp. They allowed themselves to be assisted in tending their horses before joining those already eating. Filling their plates, they looked for Julie who was resting comfortably on a bed of moss. Marlo looked at the fish doubtfully. It did not always agree with her, but she was so hungry, she threw caution to the wind and ate frantically.

After everyone had eaten, the group rested. Someone was playing a guitar. Another rider joined with a harmonica. The horses, also fed, were making crunching noises in the background. Marlo and three other riders prepared to go home. Horse trailers were brought up on the road to transport horses that might not be in sound enough condition to continue the last leg of the journey. Also, some of the riders planned to do only a portion of the ride. They, too, had made arrangements to have their trailers waiting. Marlo needed to get home for an appointment the following day. Tish wished they could have talked longer in private. Although she didn't show it, she was shocked at Marlo's admission and couldn't help wondering who the married man was.

After Marlo and the others had left, Tish lay back on a cushion of pine needles and promptly began to doze. She was not sure how long she had been asleep when she woke to find a man lying only a few yards from her, his head leaning against a saddle. It looked like a scene from an old western movie. It was Neil Darren and he was looking directly at her. Suddenly, Tish became conscious of her appearance. She knew she must look frightful. Trying to arrange her unruly hair, she felt pine needles entangled in it. Neil, watching her, got up and came to sit beside her and began pulling the needles from her hair.

Embarrassed, Tish could only think of his unmitigated gall in becoming so personal. "I can manage, thank you." she said, trying to dismiss him. She could feel the blood rushing to her cheeks with the inevitable blush that always accompanied her embarrassment.

"You look as though you've been in the wilderness," Neil looked directly into her eyes.

Startled by her own feelings, Tish attempted polite conversation, "When did you buy the Jones place?"

"About six months ago."

"But I saw you for the first time only weeks ago. I thought I saw the entire population of this place at least once a month. I'm surprised I didn't run into you before. If I had, I assure you I would have known better than to trespass. Around here, we're used to people being friendly," Tish tried to put some finality to her voice. She hoped the man who was studying her so coldly would take the hint and leave her alone.

Unaffected, Neil said confidently, "I have spent the last six months in the fields. If you hadn't been trespassing that day, I suppose our first meeting would have been today."

Tish winced at the word trespassing. She had to admit she liked to listen to the softer pronunciation of his middle Tennessee brogue. It contrasted pleasingly with the harsh flat quality of the valley residents. "Why did you choose this part of the state?" she asked, genuinely curious, "especially why Jensen's Valley?"

Neil related how he had traveled as a youngster with his father to visit Pa Ferguson and the Jones family. They were friends of long standing. "I remember thinking then that the mountains looked like giants guarding the flat fields between them. I decided then I would buy the Jones farm when I grew up, not realizing how unlikely a goal that was. As I grew older, I saw the price of land go higher and higher. I began to doubt ever being able to own a farm of any kind, anywhere, much less one in Jensen's Valley. As long as I can remember, I worked, saving every penny possible. My father used to tell people that he had a little strapling who would do anything for a dollar. I reckon the word got out, and I was hired to do every odd chore imaginable." Neil was staring into the past as he twirled a pine needle between his fingers. "I guess I broke almost every contrary horse in three counties," He grinned, remembering all the times he had hit the ground. "My folks had a small farm, we raised a few cattle and some horses. I had plenty of extra time for helping other people put up hay, build fences and that sort of thing. When I was in high school, I had a savings account, only it was earning more ambition than interest. That's when I really got lucky, I met a man from Nashville who had just retired. He bought the place next to ours. Lucky for me, he loved horses and had the money to finance his interest. He set out to have the very best and that's where I came in, as his scout. He had me out beating the bushes for a certain kind of mare. He wanted descendants of the first walking horse, Brantley's Roan Allen. Since practically all walking horses go way back to that line, the pedigree had to be narrowed down to the most desirable characteristics and conformation. He had a theory he was determined to prove and he made me a proposition. If I agreed to work for him every day after school helping him with his horses, he would pay me minimum wage plus a percentage of all the colts he sold. Well, I didn't have to think about it long. Fortunately for me, I was right there in Middle Tennessee where the breed started, the Brantley family was still raising horses not too far from where I lived. I spent a lot of time talking to Mr. French Brantley about finding the best mares. Mr. Barrett ended up buying several that he recommended."

Neil gazed into the distance, seeing into the past.

"I saw something really special in his first crop of colts. They would all scamper across the fields in the same gait, that smooth running walk that would cover ground in a hurry. He didn't breed all the mares with the same stallion, but oddly enough, all the colts looked very much alike. He'd spend hours studying their pedigrees. He made charts outlining the desirable genetic factors, undesirable ones, and noted every minute characteristic. Old Mr. Barrett was a happy man. He felt his theory was working. We gave the foals good feed, exercise, vitamins, and just watched them grow. They developed into the most mature yearlings I'd ever seen. I walked through plenty of boots halter breaking them and getting them ready for the sales. By that time there was another crop of foals on the ground. The boss-picked out one of the stud yearlings to keep. We put the other eighteen up for sale. I couldn't believe the money they brought. See, Tennessee Walking horses were getting more popular and well known all over the country. They were always popular in Hollywood because actors who couldn't sit a trot could look good on a Walker. Of course most spectators never knew what kind of horses they were. Anyway, one of our yearlings sold for $18,000. The others brought anywhere between $10 and $15,000. So, as a result of our agreement, my percentage of that first sale was $16,000."

"Aren't you two coming?" Pa's resonant voice

brought Neil and Tish to the present. Looking around, Tish saw that Pa's question had focused the attention of the entire group on them. She was conscious of the eyes following them as Neil slung his saddle over his shoulder with one hand and picked up hers with the other. Why did he assume he should help her when she was perfectly capable of carrying her own saddle? He placed the saddle on Ginger's back, making sure the blankets under it were smooth, then cinched the girth before leaving Tish to go to his own horse. Already mounted, the other riders picked up the trail on the far side of the area. Since Neil and Tish were the last to saddle up, they were also the last to leave the clearing. They rode along together. Despite her confused feeling about him, Tish was eager to hear more about the Barrett horses. Idealistically, she enjoyed success stories.

"Finish telling me what happened that brought you to the valley," she said.

"In the eyes of a high school boy, you can imagine how large a $16,000 check looked," he was smiling. "I didn't even want to put it in the bank; I just wanted to sit and look at it and feel it. To this day, I can remember every detail. Anyway," Neil paused as if he were looking at that check, "my dream of owning my own farm began to take a hopeful shape. I knew the money I had was only a drop in the bucket, but I had enough hope to make up the difference. I kept working for Mr. Barrett.

He probably wouldn't have been so good to me had he not been such a wealthy man. The most important thing to him at that time was the pure enjoyment he got from experimenting with his theory of genetics and his appraisal of what kind of colt would make the best natural show horse. Also, he seemed to enjoy my company. Every year, we watched his yearlings top the sales. They had the look of winners and, I suppose, people just couldn't stop bidding. They ended up all over the country. Still, Mr. Barrett managed to keep up with them, knowing how every one of them turned out. When the first bunch were two years old, some of them were winning at the big shows. The yearling that he kept from that first group was put in training with an outstanding trainer, Although he was capable of going to the major shows, Mr. Barrett made sure he was shown only at the little one-nighters that didn't attract much publicity. He and the trainer argued endlessly about that, but Mr. Barrett insisted on bringing the horse on slowly, not wanting to put any pressure on him. Well, to make a long story a little shorter, that horse ended up becoming Reserve Champion of the World. By that time, Mr. Barrett was more interested in another one of his colts so he sold the Reserve Champion for a big price. He gave me the promised percentage and that, plus what I had saved, was a big start on my goal of buying a farm. I graduated from high school, and, although I intended on working for him full time, he told me if

I didn't go to college, he would fire me, so I went. Naturally, I majored in Animal Science in Agriculture." Neil looked at Tish, "I'm putting you to sleep with my long story, aren't I?"

"No, go one, please," Tish was fascinated.

"After I graduated, I went back to work for Mr. Barrett. We became really worried about what was happening in the walking horse industry. For some unknown reason, trainers and exhibitors started making the horses do what was and is called 'the big lick' which amounts to hunkering down on their haunches while they raise their front feet real high in an exaggerated motion. It is still smooth, still a four-beat gait, with nodding of the head but a total exaggeration of the natural gait the horses are born with. Unfortunately, it is caused from pain; trainers sore the horses and use weights to make them step higher and reach further to delay putting their feet down. A little weight might not cause injury, but too much weight does. Anyway, we found out how bad some of the horses were being treated and became heartsick over it. Mr. Barrett started lobbying for anti-soring legislation and penalties, but it is so hard to get anything done. Lots of people who love the horses and cheer for them think they are just trained to step that way. People just don't realize." Neil paused, shaking his head, then continued.

"So, we stopped selling our horses for show and began selling them for trail riding and general pleasure. Mr. Barrett didn't need to make money anyway, but I did, so he gave me a raise and we began protesting the abuse of the show horses. I was still working there when I heard about the death of Mr. Jones. My father and I came to the valley for the funeral. I hadn't seen the place in years, but it was just as I remembered. I tried to find out who had inherited the place and was told the entire estate was tied up in a legal mess because of liens, confusion as to who was the closest kin, conflicting wills. It was several years before the place was officially offered for sale. The day of the auction, I came with my heart in my throat. Since it was such a large farm, I feared it would be subdivided into tracts. The auction seemed to last an eternity, but I came out of it the owner." Neil smiled in satisfaction. "Now every penny I ever earned or hope to earn is tied up in it. I'm up to my gizzard for the machinery and crop loan. This first year can break me if it's a bad one."

Tish was beginning to understand the protectiveness he felt for his property. "Why did you decide to gamble everything when you could have invested in something smaller with less worry?"

"The Jones place was my rainbow, I guess. I know, most people say horses are a rich man's past time, but they, along with the land, are what I love. And, I figure there are always going to be other people who love them so I plan to diversify my farming operation. I will grow mostly hay, corn, and oats, and lots of pasture. I'm going to put run-in sheds in small fields so I can pasture board horses. Pa has encouraged me to do that. He said he has to turn away people who want to pasture board because he doesn't have enough acreage. So, we're going to work together on that. He thinks there's a future in taking city people on trail rides, sort of like this one, probably with fewer miles. I don't expect to get rich, but I expect to live happy, once I get this place paid off. If I have to sell part of it, I will, but I want to see if I can keep it all." He let out a big sigh.

"I understand," Tish said, knowing now why he had been so protective of his field. She tried to picture him as a boy. She could envision a boy working, all of his spare time, working . . . she wondered if he had ever found time to play. Stopping, they drank from a spring. He held Ginger while she filled her canteen with the icy water. When she reached for Ginger's reins, she felt his hand over hers provoking sudden tension to charge through her body. She wondered why he shattered her nerves. Although she liked being with him, she was strangely threatened by his presence. Feeling his arms encircle her waist, she looked up to find his face close to her. Her eyes were caught by his sure cool gaze. Then his hard, confident lips were on hers. It was as if she had been living for that moment all her years.

"Tish," he whispered, "I feel as if I have known you all my life."

Twisting away, she swung into the saddle on

Ginger's back before turning to look at Neil, trying to compose herself.

"I'll race you to the other riders," she said, challenging him. She needed to run, to let the feelings inside her subside. She had to get away so he wouldn't notice the emotions he had stirred in her. She needed space around her to calm her thoughts. It was true that she had hoped to meet a special kind of man someday, but she had never in her wildest dreams prepared herself for the sudden and confusing storm that swirled within her. She allowed Ginger to run along a rugged trail, something she would not normally do, and plunge into a narrow creek, jumping a log that had fallen across the path. She was surprised and disappointed at how quickly she caught up to the other riders.

Neil had not attempted to catch her. Contentedly he watched Tish with her wild flying hair ahead of him and remained behind as she picked her way past several of the riders, slowing to a walk. Pa had pulled up and was removing a pebble that had become wedged in the horse's right front foot. His eyes were twinkling as he saw that Tish and Neil had rejoined the group. They stopped to see if his horse was lame, then the three of them continued up the slope which was growing steeper. They dismounted to lead their horses over several yards of rough terrain. The walk gave them an opportunity to stretch their legs before climbing back in the saddle.

CHAPTER TEN

Alex Morgan stared at the early frost on the grass several stories down from the hospital room where his son lay sleeping. When he had come to Chicago, he had assumed it would be for only a few days. If his small son had come to him any other time complaining of pains in his side and stomach, he probably would have heeded the danger signals. But it had been the night before the funeral of the child's grandmother, and it was not unusual for Jerry to complain of aches and pains. Alex assumed the discomfort was caused by the stress of the unpleasant situation; the confrontation with death, funeral parlors, unknown relatives, and grief in the faces around him. Later, when he had seen his young son crying during the funeral service, he had been touched by the sensitivity the boy obviously felt for a grandmother he hardly knew. It was not

143

until much later that he realized there was really something physically wrong with the child. After the trip to the emergency room and a diagnosis of acute appendicitis, he had waited with Mary, each chiding themselves for the delay of their responses to the obvious need of their son. Because of the delay, the appendix had ruptured. Although Jerry made a remarkable recovery from his ordeal, the rupture had forced them to stay in Chicago much longer than they intended. Alex was immensely relieved when the doctor told them it would be all right for Jerry to travel. His spirits began to soar when he realized that he would soon be on the road home . . . to Marlo. Even during the agonizing worry about his son, Alex had been unable to put Marlo out of his mind. He had become increasingly more restless as each day passed and brought the boy closer to recovery. Everything had been prepared for the trip. A small mattress, normally used for camping, had been placed in the back of the station wagon for Jerry to rest on during the long drive. He would be home sometime on October third, if nothing else happened to delay them.

Marlo had gone directly home after the ride. Tired, but pleasantly relaxed, she stretched out across her bed and napped. When she awoke, she noticed it was five o'clock already. Hunger prompted her to the refrigerator where she found chicken and potato salad. Margaret always left plenty of food prepared if she left early, as she had that day. After eating, she enjoyed a long bath. Dressing leisurely, she decided that a walk would be good for her. She meandered down the long driveway, through the estate and into the wide street that led through the exclusive residential area. Only a handful of homes were carefully placed there, well secluded by rows of evergreens, wide expanses of lawn, tennis courts, and swimming pools. Marlo strolled randomly without purpose. Hearing a strange noise, she turned. The rickety, sputtering sound was coming from an old truck. One fender was missing, and mud disguised the color of the paint used sometime in the far distant past.

Recognizing Marlo as a friend of Tish Jamison, Emmett creaked the pathetic vehicle to a halt, calling out to Marlo, "Miss Scott, have you seen Miss Tish today?"

"Why yes, I saw her this morning. She's still on the Mountain Ride," Marlo answered politely.

"Of course, I forgot about the ride or I'd a knowed where she was." Emmett chuckled at his forgetfulness. "Listen, Miss Scott, I shore would appreciate it if you'd give this letter to her for me. It's from my nephew in college." Emmett swelled with pride, smiling widely displaying two gold teeth. "Miss Tish has been askin' about him. I know she'll want to read the letter and I expect you'll be see'n her before I do."

"Why certainly, Emmett," Marlo said, feeling

useful. She accepted the letter, not noticing the car that passed.

"And this is for you, Miss Scott, for your trouble," Emmett handed Marlo a brown paper bag containing a quart of fox grape wine. Emmett knew that just about everybody in the valley appreciated his wine, even if they didn't take to his moonshine.

"Why, thank you very much, "Marlo said, touched by his thoughtfulness.

"Bye now," Emmett waved and drove on.

Although he and Marlo were going in the same direction, he knew it would not be proper for him to offer her a ride. People like her who didn't have to walk, liked to walk for fun. He had finished making his deliveries of his special wine and was now heading home to Crazy Creek.

Marlo watched the old truck clank into the distance at about the same time she approached the property line of the Scott estate. Cutting across the grounds, she entered the big lonely house. Deciding to sample some of Emmett's wine she sipped it slowly, discovering why it was rather famous throughout the valley. She drank another glass and felt a nice warm glow. The taste of the deep red liquid was not unpleasant. Lying back in a recliner, thoughts drifted to Joseph. He had been gone only a few days but she was lonely without him already, a yearning kind of lonesomeness, knowing they'd be together soon. She could dream of the wedding and their future together.

As soon as Alex saw his son settled in his bedroom he announced that he was going out to check on things in the valley. With the ambiguous explanation behind him, he drove directly to the Scott estate. He parked in a wooded area adjacent to the property as he had in the past in case Marlo had company when he arrived. Walking toward the house, he found his feet could not move fast enough. Geez, . . . how he had longed for this moment. He knew that her parents had left, going back to Florida. He let himself fantasize how he would find Marlo. He didn't care where she was or what she was doing, he was going to find her and hold her to him. Never again would he allow her to go away from him.

He entered the side door which led into the music room where Marlo spent much of her time. He was not disappointed, for he saw her there reclining in a lounge chair, so beautiful even in slacks and a sweater. The sight of her made him almost breathless with anticipation. Marlo had not heard him enter. Now, he stood before her and reached for her. She opened her eyes and saw him. She screamed. He saw how badly he had frightened her.

"Darling," he said, "I didn't mean to scare you. I just wanted to look at you. It's been so long." He pulled her to her feet and crushed her against him.

"Alex, stop, you're hurting me," Marlo gasped. Confusion clouded her thinking. She had been trying to decide what to tell Joseph about Alex but she

147

had not given any thought at all about having to face Alex, thinking he surely knew about her engagement.

"I'm sorry I had to be away for so long," he was saying, "I came just as soon as I got back."

Marlo began to realize that he didn't know. She remembered how busy Tish had been trying to do his job as well as her own because of something about his son.

"Marlo, I can't live without you. I've decided to divorce Mary so we can marry and be together all the time. Oh, I love you more than anything in the world." He was trying to kiss her.

"Stop!" Marlo shouted, pushing him from her. "Alex, I've fallen in love; I'm engaged!" she held her hand to show him the ring on her finger. "I'm sorry, Alex, I thought I loved you, but I was just lonely. I guess I used you as much as you used me, but we both knew it was wrong." Marlo's voice faltered as she saw the look on Alex's face. His temples were pounding, as blood coursed through his veins.

Alex was startled at how quickly hate could replace love. All he could feel was the rejection which lashed out at him as if he were being whipped.

"How can you turn me off like some damned machine!" he yelled. "I was willing to sacrifice everything for you . . . .everything I am. You're nothing but a rich bitch who gets her kicks from turning a man wrong side out! You can't do this to me. If I can't have you, no one will!"

Tears welled up in Marlo's eyes. The hurtful words jarred her. "Alex," she sobbed, "I'm sorry, I never meant to hurt you, but I love Joseph."

Perhaps it was the pity in her voice or the jealous rage he felt in hearing her say the name of the man she loved, he wasn't reasoning why, but he had an overwhelming urge to stop the words from coming. He grabbed Marlo around the throat, shaking her as he tightened his grip. Her small fists pounded against him, growing weaker with each blow; then they were still, dropping to her sides. Harder and harder he pressed until he felt her body grow slack. As he released his grip, she fell to the floor. Bending over her, Alex tried to see if she was dead. He couldn't be sure.

His hands started to shake. "God, what have I done!" He started to cry. Then, panic gripped him and he knew he had to get away. He stopped to wipe the door knob with his handkerchief. He looked again at Marlo; she had not moved. She must be dead. He saw nothing but a letter that had fallen from Marlo's pocket. Not touching it, Alex succumbed to his panic and fled.

CHAPTER ELEVEN

The trail riders had gathered on the crest of a high mountain; their destination. They were awed by the smoky beauty in the distance beyond them and the layers of forest below. Surrounded by a mass of russet browns, dazzling yellows, amber and oranges, the October forest was alive with an orchestra of silent music for the eyes. They would camp here. Some of them went fishing in nearby streams, while others merely feasted on the majestic view. Later there would be quiet talk about the camp fire, songs and laughter.

Hours passed as camp was leisurely set up. Several of the men gathered firewood, while others pitched tents for those who would seek shelter from the starry night. As much as Tish was intrigued by Neil Darren, she was thankful for the activity that took her away from him. She needed some time to recuperate from the jostle of her emotions. She wondered how much she was being influenced by her friends' recent engagements. Was she subconsciously trying to feel the same way they were feeling? She had, of course, been kissed before, so, what was it about Neil's kiss? Her thoughts continued to wander.

The unseasonable warm October day left its mark in sweat and dirt on the riders. Julie and Tish took soap and towels from their saddle bags and walked downstream so they could clean up in privacy. They giggled as Julie commented that they were bathing pretty close to the fishermen.

Neil was bent over a tent stake, but their departure was not unnoticed.

"I'm so hot I'm going in for a swim," Julie said as they approached a wide pool in the stream.

"Me too," Tish said.

They pulled off their soiled garments and plunged into the icy mountain water. The shock of the water, always cold, gripped both of them.

"Oh, I can't take this long!" shuddered Julie.

"Funny how we always forget how really cold this water is. I've never been so cold in my life," Tish said between chattering teeth. Hurriedly lathering her body, Tish swam numbly to the shore, allowing the current to rinse her. The pebbles felt warm as she walked to her towel. Tish put on her one change of clothing. "Now I feel like a million dollars."

"Likewise," said Julie, "but we must remember never to swim again in this running ice water. We must be getting old, Tish, because when we were kids, we liked it."

Refreshed, they rested on the shore in the last glow of sunlight through the filter of crimson leaves.

"Tish Jamisen and Neil Darren make a very attractive couple," Julie teased. "Don't you agree?"

"Now stop that, Julie. Don't jump to any conclusions. After all, I hardly know him."

"You like what you see, don't you?"

"Of course. I have to admit he is a looker."

Julie smiled, "I'm glad there's someone new in these parts. Now that Marlo and I are getting married, we won't have to feel guilty about abandoning our dear friend."

"Julie," Tish protested, "just because we rode together part of the time on this ride doesn't mean that we'll be seeing each other after we get down off the mountain. Besides, I'm not sure I would want to see too much of him."

"Whatever you say," Julie said, knowing she had not imagined the vibrations between Neil and Tish. They walked lazily back to the campsite. Julie wished her Jimmy enjoyed riding as much as she did, but it was all right for them to have separate interests. They did enough together.

The evening passed pleasantly. Tish found herself seated by Neil around the fire. He did not talk directly to her, focusing his attention on the group at large. When she finally rose to retire for the night, he merely nodded his goodnight along with the others. Tish and Julie spread their bedrolls in the same tent they had slept in every ride for the past dozen years.

"This ground gets harder every year," grumbled Julie.

"Do you suppose our age has anything to do with it?" laughed Tish.

"No, never!"

"Do you remember the first time we came?" Tish asked.

"I'll never forget it," Julie said. "We felt so grown-up until the sun went down. After dark, we weren't so brave. Remember that old screech owl?"

"I had never been so scared in my life." Tish remembered the sound of the owl.

They continued to reminisce about past rides, promising each other that nothing would ever stop them from attending all the future rides so long as they could swing a leg over the back of their horses.

"I'm not going to be one of those wives who never does anything without her husband," Julie said. "I think it's important for married people to continue to do some things individually. Don't you?"

"Yes." Tish thought Julie would make a good wife, never overly dependent. Her thoughts wandered back to Marlo. She wished Marlo had stayed on the ride. Looking at her watch, Tish saw that it was only a little after nine. It seemed much later.

Her eyelids grew heavy. An image of Neil Darren passed through her mind and then she was asleep. Julie was already dreaming of her wedding day.

The residents of Jensen's Valley were greeted by a splendid autumn morning as they stirred from their sleep on Saturday, the third day of October. Margaret Hobson washed a load of clothes before daylight. She was hanging them on the clothesline, humming a nameless tune. Bill Hobson was gathering his garden tools. Although the Scotts kept a well supplied tool shed on the estate, Bill preferred to use some of his own tools. He was fond of saying that they were used to his hands. He got into his pick-up truck and waited for Margaret. He could hear her coming before he could see her.

They rode in the truck to the Scott place. It had been this way for years; Margaret working on the inside while Bill tended the grounds. When the senior Scotts were out of town, the Hobsons went every Tuesday, Thursday, and Saturday. One of the more traditional families of the black community, Bill and Margaret were content in their jobs as domestic servants even though their grown children had left the valley for more prestigious jobs. Margaret had grown tired of her children's goading her to quit. She had gathered them around her during their last Christmas visit asking them to sit down and listen.

"Once and for all," she had explained, "I don't cook and clean houses because I'm black. I clean houses because I like to clean and I cook because I like to cook! And, I don't want to hear no more talk about Marlo Scott being uppity white. I love that girl. None of us, black or white, gets to choose our color. Now, I'm really proud of you all, that you've gotten to be so successful in your jobs. Just don't you keep badgerin' your pa and me about being old fashioned blacks. Sure, we're proud of all the important things black people can do nowadays, but we want to keep on doing what we know and like. Is that understood?"

The children nodded. They never again attempted to get their parents to quit their jobs.

As the truck came nearer to the estate, Margaret said, "This shore is a fine morning, ain't it?"

"Yes, Marg, it is. I'm anxious to see how those chrysanthemums are doing." Bill spoke with earnest anticipation. He loved tending the grounds around the estate. He enjoyed, too, the praise he received for his efforts. Everyone in the valley envied his green thumb and eye for landscaping. Bill pulled into the drive, stopping when he was in front of the garage. He began unloading his tools while his wife lifted a basket from the truck.

"I brought Miss Marlo some of our hot cinnamon rolls for breakfast," she winked at Bill. Marlo loved Margaret's baking and always insisted on her and Bill joining her for coffee. Margaret let herself in the kitchen door. Bill started walking toward the bed of chrysanthemums when a terrifying scream stopped him in his tracks. Turning, he saw his Marg running and falling from the kitchen door. He dropped the tools he was carrying and ran to her.

"What is it?" he demanded.

Margaret's mouth was open but no sound came. She pointed to the house. Bill shook her, but couldn't get a word. All she could do was point to the house. He left to go inside as Margaret fell on the ground in a heap. sobs rocking her massive body. "Poor little Marlo, poor little thing," she found her voice and muttered to herself.

Bill saw Marlo's body as it lay on the floor in the music room and tears began to run down his face. Fighting to control the shock, his mind was filled with flashes from the past. Marlo as a toddler, waddling after him, calling him Bill-Bill. Little Marlo, picking the flowers he had grown. Little Marlo, clinging to him at the end of a day, saying, "Take me with you, Bill-Bill, please." The blond child when she first became fully aware of the color of his skin, rubbing a finger across his face, asking him why it was dark. Focusing on Marlo now, as she lay rigid on the floor, her fingers outstretched in a pleading helpless gesture, he saw that her eyes were open wide in terror stilled by death. Her mouth was shouting a silent scream. Bill wanted to run as Marg had done, but he forced himself to go to the phone in the kitchen. As he dialed the Sheriff's office, Bill doubted he would be able to speak, but he did.

"Miss Marlo's been killed," he sobbed into the receiver.

"Where?" was the frantic reply.

"The house . . . the Scott house. Please hurry." Bill hung up the phone and returned to the yard to find Margaret crying in the grass. He sat down beside her, cradling her in his arms, both of them weeping.

The sheriff and a number of his deputies arrived quickly. Although there were a goodly number of disturbances in the area, when people yelled and fought with each other, murder was uncommon. Bill and Marg provided the authorities no clues. No, they had touched nothing. No, they didn't know who Marlo had seen yesterday. Sheriff Tompkins had not noticed the letter at first. He wondered how he could have missed it when later he did. He guessed it was the sick feeling he had experienced when he first saw her body. Reminding himself that he was the sheriff, he told himself he was supposed to stay strong and not turn to jelly at the sight of a victim. Nevertheless, his vision had blurred when he saw Marlo. Although there wasn't the blood and distortion of many of the traffic fatalities he had seen, there was something eerie about the expression on Marlo's face. Her golden hair seemed to frame and focus attention on her face.

Sheriff Tompkins picked up the letter and noted the address. The letter had been mailed to Emmett Moss. His temples began to throb as his mind leaped at the evidence. There was no one he would rather arrest than Emmett. He turned to see the wine bottle, more than half empty. Gingerly picking it up with a handkerchief, he smelled the contents. It was most definitely the product of Emmett. No one else could make wine out of foxgrapes, he thought, A smile began to twist the corners of his mouth. Sheriff Tompkins had never forgiven Emmett for making a fool of him the morning of the raid. Impatiently he waited for the completion of photographs. At last, the coroner arrived. He was also the family physician. He had been delivering a baby when he was summoned to the scene. Finally, the mortician was able to remove the body and a guard was posted to prevent the admission of the curious or thieves.

The riders had gotten an early start on Saturday morning. The cooling air of the mountains filled the horses with enthusiasm for the journey home. The remainder of the ride was a shorter trail down the mountain than the one they had climbed. Since the trail home was a descending one, the horses did not tire as easily as they did when they were climbing. Nevertheless, they had to be careful lest they slide on the steeper portions of the trail. They had traveled some distance when they were startled to see a rider headed full stride up the slope towards them. Tish recognized the boy astride the horse as one of Pa's stable hands. Both he and the horse were breathless as they rushed to Pa.

"Pa," he caught his breath, "Mrs. Ferguson sent me to fetch you." He paused again.

"Speak up, son. What is it?" Fear showed in Pa's eyes. A dozen possible tragedies raced through his mind.

"It's Miss Marlo Scott . . .she's been murdered!"

Tish heard the words. She wanted to pull them from her ears and throw them back into the boy's mouth. "No," she said, barely audible. Neil turned just in time to see her grow limp and fall from the saddle. Leaping from his horse, he caught her in his arms. She was faintly aware of him as the sky began to come into focus. Gasping at the foul-smelling ammonia someone had brought along, she gradually regained her senses. "What happened?" she asked.

"You fainted and fell off your horse."

"No, I never faint." She was surprised. Then she recalled what the boy had said. Voices from the group sounded like a collective swarm of bees as everyone spoke and gasped in astonishment. Then came the questions, sorrow, anger, disbelief and speculation. Aware now that she was lying with her head in Neil's lap, Tish tried to sit up.

"Shh, be still a minute," he spoke to her in the same tones he had used on the spooky horse he had been riding. She lay quietly letting the situation arrange itself in her mind. She heard Pa addressing the riders.

"We'll just ride on in as quickly as possible, but slow enough that we don't abuse our horses. We'll stop long enough to rest and water the horses, but we won't make camp. I'll pass around some snacks that you all can eat on horseback when you're hungry. If you need to stop, that's fine."

The riders began moving again, down the slope, most in silence.

"Do you feel like riding now?" Neil asked Tish. He watched her shake her head to affirm that she did. "I'll walk for awhile," he said, "and lead both horses." Lifting her from the ground into the saddle, Neil began the trip home.

Tish saw Julie sobbing hysterically into Pa's shoulder. Tish wondered why she wasn't crying herself. She thought of Clyde Ramsey who had been killed by a shotgun and wondered how Marlo had been killed. Shuddering, she didn't want to ask. "I can manage Ginger, Neil, really . . . you go ahead."

Neil gave Ginger's reins to Tish but continued to walk beside her. The last miles were covered silently. Neil did not mount his horse until they reached the meadow. At the stables, he put both horses in a corral after carefully rubbing them down. Tish was expressionless. She was relieved to see her parents waiting for her.

"Marlo, Tish, and Julie were like sisters," Tish's mother explained to Neil who kept a watchful eye on Tish. He nodded his head in understanding. He would have to wait before he could know Tish better. Neil hadn't known Marlo, yet he could sense the loss of one of the valley's well-loved daughters. In small towns and communities, each death seemed significant to almost everyone.

Marlo's distraught parents had flown back from Florida on a chartered plane. When they were trying to make arrangements for the funeral, Mrs. Scott was near hysteria but adamant.

"I never want to look at my daughter's face in a box . . . that's all a coffin is . . . a box! I want her laid out in her big canopy bed. That's how I want people to remember her, a beautiful sleeping princess. We'll let everyone come here to see her, then they can put her in a casket just before the funeral. It will be closed. Do you understand?"

The undertaker was bewildered. He had never been asked to do anything so unusual. Hesitantly, he looked at Mr. Scott.

"If that's what she wants, then that's the way it will be," Mr. Scott's voice was final. He was too hurt too care about the details of the burial. He was desperately trying to focus on the fact that her spirit had left the body and was now in a better place.

Years ago, it was fairly common for wakes to be held in the homes of the deceased. Some people in Crazy Creek and the valley held onto old ways, so no one was shocked at the decision made by the Scotts to have Marlo brought home. They would not know, however, until they filed past her that she would be lying in a bed instead of a coffin.

The evening that the family was to receive friends, the grounds of the estate were filled with people long before the appointed hour. Tish, accompanied by her parents drove to the house through the crowd, wondering how many had come out of curiosity.

They had her big canopy bed brought downstairs and placed in the music room which was her favorite place. Also, there were two doors which made it easy for mourners to file past, in one door off the front hall and out the other to exit also through the wide entrance hall and front door.

When Tish entered the room, she was glad of Mrs. Scott's decision. The huge bed, canopied by white eyelet and skirted with yards of matching flounce, had bed curtains of sheer mesh which were pulled back and sashed with white satin bows; it did truly provide a regal setting for a sleeping princess. Marlo's expression was now serene. Her blonde curls were arranged carefully on a satin pillow. A white spread was tucked lightly about her waist. In her hands, clasped together, was a single red rose. She had been dressed in a soft white gown fashioned with lace on the high yoke which covered the bruised neck. Flanking the bed were some of the floral arrangements, carefully chosen from many to represent Marlo's closest friends. Tish heard a number of people gasp as they entered the room. The spacious, tastefully furnished music room was awesome even under ordinary circumstances, but now was startling with the fairy princess stilled by death, lying in the bed as if she might wake and rise at any minute. Mrs. Scott sat in a rocking chair beside the bed. Her husband stood beside her. Also, standing next to the bed was Joseph, his mouth set in rigid determination, There was bitterness in his eyes. Marlo's parents burst into tears as Tish approached them. Hugging them, Tish was finally able to cry. When she left the room she saw Bill Hobson standing by the door. He, too, lost his composure when he saw her. They joined in a comforting embrace.

"Alex, we must go. What will people think?" Mary was pleading.

"Tell them I'm sick. I am, I really am." Alex spoke in earnest.

"Oh, alright, but I hate going alone." Mary finished dressing and left for the Scott home.

Alex remained lying in bed, glad to be alone. He knew he could never, under any circumstances, enter that house again. Afraid he would talk in his sleep during awful dreams, he had not slept well and was now suffering from extreme sleep deprivation. Was it guilt or fear that caused the sickening feeling that engulfed him, Alex wondered. His palms were cold but sweaty. Where the hell was his conscience when he had killed her, he asked himself. He referred to Marlo as her, not being able to form her name even in his mind. He would never be able to face her parents. How could he attend church again, as if nothing ever happened? Then, there would be Tish in the office. Getting out of the bed, Alex went to the bathroom where he fumbled through the medicine cabinet for the tranquilizers Mary sometimes took. Maybe they would help. Anything was worth a try. Swallowing one, he returned to the safety of the bed. Pulling the cover tightly over his body, Alex began to think about the bed. A bed was a place for sleeping and being with a woman. Never again would he be able to do either. Alex hated himself. He wondered if he would learn to live with his guilt. It seemed doubtful. What should he do? No, he could not and would not confess. He'd rather kill himself. Considering the possibility of suicide, he surveyed the many possible ways of taking his life. Picturing his body after a gun had been fired at his temple, he shuddered. Then, he considered slashing his wrists. He envisioned blood all over the bathroom floor and felt queasy. It would have to be pills, he decided, but, not yet. First he would suffer long enough to see if the guilt would pass. He would see. The tranquilizer had taken effect allowing a relaxed Alex to drift into sleep.

The funeral hour was near. Tish noticed Bill sitting at the very back of the church. He looked exhausted. Margaret had been ordered to bed because her blood pressure had climbed dangerously high. The faithful couple had held a vigilant wake

for Marlo. They had been eager to serve their em-
ployers' every need, trying somehow to assuage the
terrible grief. After the house was empty and silent
from the departure of the last friends, Margaret had
persistently coaxed Mrs. Scott into bed. Mrs. Scott
had succumbed to her gentle prodding. Then, it was
only Margaret and Bill alone by Marlo's bed where
they remained the rest of the night. Weeping and
praying, they grieved in their own way. They recalled the many times they had taken Marlo's hand-
me-down clothes to their own daughters. Now, as
Bill sat in the pew of the church, he was still without
sleep, having been on duty since the body had been
found.

The service began. The minister droned on in his
whispery voice, eulogizing Marlo as a loving daughter, a gifted generous person who had been
privileged to enjoy a fulfilling, although short, life.
As she listened, she recognized the unmistakable
sound of quiet snoring. Heads were turning. There
were critical glares towards the rear of the church.
Tish saw Bill from the corner of her eye. His head
was resting against the back wall of the church.
From his open mouth came the sound of heavy
breathing and faint snoring. Tish's emotions plum-
meted in a somersault of responses. She wanted to
both laugh and cry. Her feelings were as inappro-
priate as Bill's sleep. No one ever fell asleep at a
funeral. The irony of it, Tish knew, was the criticism
Bill would receive from some, when no one in at-

tendance, not Marlo's parents, not Julie nor Tish herself, had loved Marlo more than Bill. The dependable servant had been Marlo's most reliable ally, the one person on whom she always relied.

"Poor old soul," Tish muttered, "he is so exhausted, sleep reached out to rescue him." She wished she could go to him and clasp his gnarled old hand and tell him everything would be all right, as he had done for her and Marlo when their tree house had fallen and when one of their many pets had died. Someone sitting near Bill shook him gently awake.

Thankfully, the graveside service was brief. Julie and Tish walked down the long brick lane which led from the cemetery. When they overheard the indignant voices behind them, they paused to listen.

"Ruby," Mrs. Zickle was saying, "have you ever seen anything so rude in all your life as that . . . her own servant going to sleep!"

"No," Tish's Aunt Ruby agreed, "after all those years of steady employment . . . why, you'd think he'd show some respect from appreciation if for no other reason."

Tish, bristling, turned to face the ladies. "Did you sleep last night?" Not waiting for a reply, she continued coldly, "I'm sure you did, but Bill Hobson didn't. He spent the entire night standing watch over Marlo's body. Did you know he waited outside the funeral home while her body was being prepared? Figure out how many hours he has been by her side and remember that he is an old man. Now, who do you think is being rude and disrespectful?"

Glaring into the bewildered face of her aunt, Tish was satisfied to see a small clouding of shame. She turned to Julie and they walked from the cemetery. This was the first time they had been alone since the news of Marlo's death.

"That was the saddest funeral that I have ever attended," Julie said.

"I know," Tish responded.

"What are we going to do, Tish? I don't think I'm going to be able to concentrate on my job, and I sure don't want to plan my wedding. I feel guilty because I can go on with mine and she can never have hers," Julie begins sobbing. "I think all the tears have been shed then here I go again."

They sat in silence for a few minutes, lost in their own thoughts and grief before Tish spoke, "I am going to the office tomorrow and try to get my mind on other things. I don't know if I can, but I'm going to try."

CHAPTER TWELVE

Tish was so tired, she thought she would be able to sleep but throughout the night she tossed and turned in bed, falling asleep only to wake again an hour or so later. She was relieved when morning finally came. Although she had not had sufficient sleep, she was determined to go into the office.

She was the first to arrive and was sitting stoically at her desk, picking through the stack of correspondence waiting for her when Mabel entered.

"Tish, I was just going to phone you." Nodding to Alex's door, she said, "He called in sick, and I sure don't know what else to do but put it in your lap." Mabel sighed and took a deep breath before continuing, "The principal of the Grammar School called and asked if someone could pick up the Moss children. They were hurt during recess." With an incredulous expression on her face, Mabel said, "Can you imagine kids throwing rocks at little children!"

"Why?" Tish asked in astonishment.

"Because of their father, I'm sure."

"What about Emmett?"

"You haven't heard?" Mabel asked.

"Heard what?" pressed Tish,

"He killed Marlo Scott. I thought the whole town knew."

"He did not . . . he would never!" Tish was adamant.

"Well, he was arrested last night. They found a letter addressed to him . . . it was right by the body, and a bottle of wine with his fingerprints all over it. Then, on top of all of that, he was seen with Marlo only an hour or so before she was killed." Mabel seemed satisfied that she had quoted all the evidence needed to justify the arrest.

Tish stood for a moment, opened her mouth to speak, but said nothing. Instead, she turned and left the office.

By the time she walked into the principal's office, she was already angry. Then she saw the Moss children waiting there with the principal. Their sad faces were tear-streaked and showed red welts and abrasions made by rocks. Their clothes were torn and soiled with clay and blood. Tish stood looking at the children, her own cheeks flushed with the most anger she had ever felt. She turned to face the principal. "How could this happen? Where was your supervision or don't you have any?"

"Believe me Miss Jamison, I have reprimanded the teacher who was in charge. They were at recess and she stepped inside to get her sweater, when she returned to the playground, she found them throwing rocks at the children. It is dreadful. I am punishing the children responsible, but I thought the Moss children should be taken home . . . since they're hurt . . . until things cool off."

Tish hugged Penny and Jackson, then took them by the hand and led them from the office without saying another word.

Inside the Ranchero, Penny is the first to speak, "They say my daddy is a murderer."

"Well, he's not, they'll see." Tish answered.

As Tish braked to a stop in front of the Moss place, Penny and Jackson leaped from the car and ran up the steps into the waiting apron of their mother.

Looking at the children, Mattie told them, "It's goin' to be alright. Go in the house and change your clothes and then get yourselves some molasses cookies there in the kitchen. Thelma is in there, she'll help you. I need to talk to Miss Tish about your daddy."

Penny and Jackson nodded and ran into the house. Mattie waved Tish into a chair on the porch, then sits wearily in a nearby rocker.

"I've been sittin' here for hours, just a rockin', feelin' so helpless. I knowed I shouldn't a sent them little ones to school, but I just couldn't think this mornin'. They got up all bright and happy, ready to catch the bus." Shaking her head, Mattie continued, "The older children, they knew last night, so I let them stay home. But, Penny and Jackson . . . they're so young . . . I thought they could maybe go along as usual."

Tish said as reassuringly as she could, "I'm going to do everything I can to help. I am just so sorry I didn't know that he was charged before all of this happened."

Mattie looked at Tish with newly found hope, "Oh, I'm so relieved to hear you say that. I was a'feared you'd think he done it. On top of all the evidence they found, he came home drunker than an owl that night, the night of the murder. I hate to say it, Miss Tish, but I can see why they think he done it." Mattie burst into tears.

"Does he have a lawyer yet?" Tish asked.

"No, but they'll appoint a public defender."

"If I can get my father to take the case, would that be alright with you?" Tish asked.

"Oh, that would be wonderful, thank you, thank you." She reached for Tish's hands and clasped them. "Miss Tish, no matter what happens, I'll be obliged to you for the rest of my days."

Tish got up, gave Mattie a hug and said, "I'm going to talk to Dad right now."

Tish drove straight to her parents' home, knowing her father would probably be in his study. She found him where she expected him to be, seated in front of a fireplace quietly studying the flames.

"Daddy . . ."

"I've already taken Emmett's case." Charles Jamison said before Tish could ask him.

"How did you know what I was going to ask?"

"I know you, daughter." he chucked softly then became serious again, "Tish, have you forgotten that I used to fox hunt with Emmett?"

"Why . . . yes, I had."

"You learn a lot about a man while you're sitting under a tree next to him, just listening to the hounds. That's why I went to see Emmett this morning. He's a strong man, but he doesn't look good. He's really taken a beating, emotionally and physically."

Tish was outraged, "I didn't think that kind of thing could happen anymore!"

"Normally it doesn't, but Tish, you have to understand human nature. The Scott family made this town feel very important. Not many little mountain towns can boast about having the state's wealthiest family as one of their own. And, you know, Marlo was thought of almost like a member of royalty."

"Yes, it used to bug me when we were kids."

As they sat thinking, Tish joined her father in searching the flames with her eyes as if looking for clues.

"What are Emmett's chances?"

"The circumstantial evidence is heavy. I'm afraid he won't have much of a chance in the lower court unless I can come up with new evidence. The Prosecutor has made some blunders so there is the possibility of discrediting some of the evidence through technicalities. Whatever way we go, it's going to be a battle. It may mean years of appeals."

Tish allowed the details of Marlo's confession of a secret affair with a married man surface in her mind. She had hoped that Marlo's secret could be buried forever. She cringed at the hurt a scandal would cause Marlo's grief stricken parents and Joseph. Yet, she knew that Emmett's life was more important than Marlo's reputation. She began telling her father what she knew, believing Marlo would want her to. When she had finished, she waited for him to speak.

"Do you have any idea who the man was, Tish?"

"No, none at all."

"Let's keep this information to ourselves for the time being. Perhaps he will reveal himself in some way. Perhaps someone saw them."

The days passed uneventfully. If Tish's father had turned up any evidence, he kept it to himself. Tish visited the Moss family as often as possible, always leaving sadder than the time before. The family had sold all of Emmett's wine. Many people in the valley, convinced that Emmett would never be free to make anymore, were stocking all they could.

The evenings were long and dreary. Tish thought of Neil Darren. It had been more than two weeks since the Mountain Ride. She tried to shrug away the disappointment she felt because he had not phoned. She thought he felt something for her when they were together on the ride. She wished she could share her grief for Marlo and her fear for Emmett with him; he seemed so understanding and comforting, but Neil would have to wait. Wait, of course, if he was even interested. As time went on, it appeared he wasn't. She had Julie, but when they talked, they ended up just as sad as they were in the beginning. And Julie had Jimmy who was a great comfort to her. His steady, no nonsense view of life provided the kind of support she needed. Tish sighed, feeling a little sorry for herself. She picked up her little terrier and hugged him. "You are my comfort, aren't you sweetie," she said to the dog who wagged his tail, happy for the attention.

Tish did not know how long she had slept before she was frightened into consciousness by a scratching at her window. Frozen, she listened, wondering if Marlo's murderer had now come for her. Again she heard the scratching. This time is was followed by a hoarse whisper.

"Miss Tish it's me, Emmett."

Tish sat up in bed and looked at the window. When she saw the blood streaked face pressed against it, she drew back in fear. The face did not look like Emmett.

"Please, Miss Tish, I got to talk to you," pleaded the now unmistakable voice of Emmett Moss.

Hurriedly, she grabbed her robe, slipping into it as she went to the door.

"Oh, dear Lord!" She gasped as the bloody figure stumbled into the room. Although she tried to put herself into action, it was as if her feet were cemented to the floor and her arms lifeless, incapable of moving. She fought desperately the impulse to faint.

Emmett, seeing her reaction, closed the door. The click of the latch seemed to bring Tish back. She helped Emmett to a kitchen chair where she examined the severe facial lacerations.

"You need stitches." she saw that most of the blood was coming from a gash above his right temple. Darting about the cottage looking for first aid equipment, she cursed herself for not having kept everything in one place. Sponging away the caked blood, she could see that one gash continued to bleed. Applying pressure to the wound, she again addressed Emmett,

"You have to have stitches."

"You'll have to sew it yourself then," Emmett said.

"No!" she shuddered, "I can't."

"Do you want me to go back to jail and get killed?"

"No . . . but, Emmett . . . I can't put in stitches. I don't know how, and I don't have proper equipment. And . . . you'd probably get blood poisoning and die anyway." Her eyes were wide. She started to cry.

"Now, Miss Tish," Emmett's voice was calm. "There's nothing to it. When I was a boy, there weren't no doctor around. I've seen my Ma sew up lots of folks.

"But she was a midwife and a herb doctor," Tish protested.

"I'll tell you what to do. Go ahead now, fetch a needle and some white thread."

Tish found herself bringing her sewing box to him.

"This here will do fine." He pulled a sewing needle and some white thread from the box.

"Thread the needle and boil them both. That'll disinfect 'em."

There was something compelling about Emmett's voice. Obediently, Tish followed his directions. While they waited for the water to boil, Emmett explained how the stitches should be made. Tish found that her fear began to subside under Emmett's calm manner.

"Don't get too close to the edges," he said, "or the thread will pull right on through the skin. You've got to take a fairly good sized bite into the skin."

"Oh . . . Emmett, I can't," Tish began to tremble. "Why don't I go get Mattie or someone you trust to do this."

Emmett sighed in exasperation looking directly at Tish with his deep eyes pleading. "I trust you. They'll probably be watching my house by now."

"All right," she almost shouted, "but if I faint, don't be surprised!" Tish took the pan off the stove wondering how she would retrieve the needle from the scalding water. Carefully, she poured the water from the pan leaving the needle to cool as she scrubbed her hands. "God, help me, please," she breathed as she hurriedly picked up the needle, anxious to get the task over with before she lost her nerve. She approached the wound as a mouse might approach a cat, gingerly, not daring a sound. Desperately trying to think of the flesh as torn pieces of fabric, Tish put the needle through an edge of the skin, then another. "There's one," she whispered.

Emmett was stoic, not daring to flinch lest he frighten Tish from the task.

"Did it hurt terribly?" Tish asked.

"No," Emmett lied, "You did just fine. Now, go on with the others."

Tish continued until the gash was closed. She made five stitches. Finished, she realized that her legs were numb. Feeling her knees begin to buckle, she clutched the edge of the table and dropped into a chair. Seconds later, the swaying motion of the room began to still.

"Have you got any liquor here?" Emmett asked.

"Yes, I've got bourbon and a few bottles of your

stuff from the raid."

"Let me have some bourbon," Emmett smiled, "and you'd better have one yourself."

Pouring the bourbon, Tish placed the glasses and the bottle on the table. She gulped the bitter liquid with haste and felt it reach from her throat to her stomach and gradually disperse to her limbs.

Her mind wheeled back to the reality of the situation, questions began to topple over each other.

"Emmett, what the hell are you doing out of jail?"

"I escaped. I had to."

"How? Why? I know you got beat up."

"Well, that old place ain't much of a jail. The mortar that holds the bars in has crumbled. I knowed I could get out the first day if I'd a wanted to, but I thought I'd wait and give your pa a chance to clear me"

"Well, go on," Tish prompted, "why'd you change your mind?"

"When they first arrested me, they beat me up pretty good. They were tryin' to get me to confess. Since I didn't do nuthin', naturally, I couldn't confess. They said they'd tell people I got in a fight tryin' to escape. Finally, they got tired, I guess. Anyway, they took me to the cell. The next morning, your pa came to see me. He asked me how I got beat up. I told him. He told the sheriff I'd been questioned illegally and that I'd probably get off because of them violating my rights. He warned them not to bother me no more."

Emmett paused to take another drink of the bourbon. "Well, I stayed up there in that cell just bidin' my time knowin' what a fine lawyer your pa is. They didn't bother me again until tonight. The sheriff and that Watkins deputy, they got to drinking in the office. I could hear them talkin'. They got louder and louder, sayin' they weren't going to let no slick lawyer tell them how to run their jail.

Then they got to bragging about how they bet they could make me talk. Well, pretty soon, they came up to my cell and started in on me. That's how I got banged up. I started fighting back. I think maybe I broke the sheriff's nose. Anyway, he backed off holdin' his nose. Watkins hit me across the head with his stick. I passed out. When I came to, I could hear them in the office again. This time they were talking about how they could kill me and make it look like I was making an escape. About that time, the Bower boy came in the office. I recognized his voice."

Tish knew Bo Bower, He was a fair minded young man.

"Bo came to my cell," Emmett continued, "He told me what I'd already heard. I could tell he was scared. He was fidgetin' around like a turkey the day before Thanksgiving. I told him I was gettin' out. He said he'd try to keep them talkin' 'till I had time to get a good start. I pulled the bars out and high-tailed it out of there. I was afraid to go home because I figured they'd look there first." Emmett sighed, exhausted from the explanation. They sat staring at each other.

Tish sought a path of action. Ideas kept stalling. No, she couldn't tell her father. He would attempt to find a legal avenue which might come too late to save Emmett. No, she couldn't harbor a fugitive on her father's property. Her cottage was on his property. No, she couldn't send Emmett back to jail to be murdered.

Emmett interrupted Tish's thoughts. I'm gonna run for it, Miss Tish. Get word to Mattie, will ya?"

"No," she said looking straight into his eyes. Something about the way he was sitting with his swollen face turned to the light reminded her of the late Mr. Freeman, someone they both knew.

"I've got it," she cried with her eyes wide with sudden inspiration.

"What?" Emmett asked eagerly.

"You can hide out at the Freeman place.

"They won't help me," Emmett protested.

"It doesn't matter. They won't have to know, and no one would ever think to look there." Quickly, Tish explained the eccentricities of the Freeman sisters. She told them they left food for the spirit of their dead father.

"If they hear you moving around, they'll just think you're the ghost. You can stay in the cellar. There is an outside and an inside entrance. The stairway in the cellar leads straight into the kitchen.

They don't lock any of their doors. I can visit you once in a while and keep you informed. I go over there pretty often anyway. It will be the perfect place."

"What if they find me?" Emmett was doubtful.

"If they go to the cellar, just duck out of sight. They'll never find you." Tish was looking out the window. It was dangerously close to dawn. Quickly, she fixed a sandwich for Emmett. Then, after bundling up some fruit and canned foods, she filled a thermos with coffee. Next, she got some blankets and a pillow. While filling her camping jug with water, she coddled the reluctant escapee into agreeing to the scheme. Emmett folded himself on the floor of the vehicle and allowed Tish to cover him with blankets and a pillow.

As she drove to the Freeman home, she remembered the night she had helped move the still. She remembered how worried she had been about getting caught. That crime would be nothing compared to this, she thought. Here she was, aiding and abetting an escaped fugitive.

"Lord, help me," she breathed, and help us get there safely. Her knee was shaking so bad she could barely shift the gears.

Tish was glad she had passed no cars before arriving safely on the Freeman property. Canopied by the dense foliage that lined the long driveway, she cut off the ignition and remained motionless for a few minutes to see if the noise of the automobile had awakened the sisters. Quietly, she ushered Emmett into the dark cellar. Lighting a candle, she held it up for him to survey the vast cluttered interior. The air was heavy with the smell of curing hams, barrels of apples, potatoes, and bunches of onions and peppers strung from the ceiling. The walls gleamed with rows of jars filled with vegetables and jellies. There were clusters of dried dill, large crocks of pickled cucumbers, and other relishes.

"Perfect," Tish exclaimed, as she discovered a cot among the piles of discarded furniture.

"You can sleep here." She put the blankets on the dusty mattress.

"No, Miss Tish," sighed Emmett, "I'd better stay awake so I can hide if someone comes in."

Tish was silent as she pondered the situation. "I've got an idea. We'll put some cans and buckets in front of both doors. If anyone opens the door, the noise will wake you before they see you. The cot is hidden from view from either door."

"Emmett grinned, "Miss Tish, you are a clever little thing. I'm glad, because I doubt if I could stay awake even if I tried."

Tish returned to her cottage in time to hear a distant rooster announcing the new day.

CHAPTER THIRTEEN

News of Emmett's escape spread like wild fire throughout the valley. The sheriff organized a search unit complete with bloodhounds. His instructions to the men were to shoot the murdering heathen on sight.

Tish was again abruptly awakened from a sound sleep. This time it was bloodhounds baying and scratching at her door.

"Good Lord," she cried feeling panic ice its way like splinters through her body.

There was a loud banging on the door accompanied by shouts. Tish knew she'd better do something before the men forced the door. She reached for her robe, then realized she was still dressed, "Oh, no," she thought, "I probably have Emmett's scent on me. And, there are those bloody bandages! "Dear

Jesus, what am I going to do!"

"Just a minute!" she yelled. "I'm coming. Quickly, she hid the bloody bandages under the sink. Bracing herself, she went to the door. Careful to allow no more than a crack lest the hounds attack her, she forced an expression of bewildered innocence as she peered coyly around the edge of the door. "Yes?"

"Miss Tish, are you all right?" Sheriff Tompkins asked excitedly. The hounds trailed that murderin' varmint here!"

"There must be some mistake, Sheriff, there's no varmint here. You can come in and see for yourself, but you'll have to leave those big old dogs outside. I can't have them messing up my house. Besides, I've got a little dog in here."

The handler pulled back the dogs to allow the sheriff inside. "If you don't mind, Miss Tish, I'd better look around to make sure he's not hiding in here. He might of come in while you were asleep."

"Go right ahead, sheriff, but I'm sure no one is here. My own dog would have barked. He is a very good watch dog. I'm afraid your dogs are a bit confused."

"Guess you're right," the sheriff shook his head after his casual search revealed nothing.

"Maybe he just came by here. He might even have tried the door."

"I guess that's quite possible." Tish tried to act amiable. "Who are you looking for Sheriff?"

"Emmett broke out," he growled.

Tish smiled through the window as she saw the men curse the dogs because they refused to pick up a scent anywhere beyond the driveway. She began to breathe normally only after the group gave up and left. At least she had a good excuse for being late to work, she thought, as she dressed hurriedly for the office.

Alex sat drumming his empty desk with the eraser of his freshly sharpened pencil. Where the hell was Tish, he wondered. She was getting too damned independent coming in whenever she damned well pleased. He would really let her have a piece of his mind if she ever got to the office. He had to get a report filed and in the mail today. There was no way he could write it without Tish. He became more angry at the realization of just how much he needed the insufferable Tish Jamison.

Tish bounced into the office at the same moment the pencil snapped in Alex's hand. Tish noticed his anger and rapidly explained what had detained her. Suddenly, in the middle of the explanation, she was rendered speechless. The shirt! That's where she had seen the shirt in Marlo's house . . . on Alex!

"What's the matter, Tish? You look like you've just seen a ghost?"

"I'm sorry, I suddenly don't feel well." Tish was unsteady on her feet. "I'm going back home."

"You can't do that!" Alex snapped, "We've got to write the quarterly report today! Geez, Tish, you know I've been waiting all week for you to help me." Alex was pleading like a child.

"Write it yourself. It's your job anyway, not mine." Tish felt good at unleashing a message so long harnessed by clinched teeth. She wheeled away from Alex and walked from the room leaving Mabel staring in disbelief.

Tish began to tremble as she drove away. She had to get away from Alex, to find some space which would allow her to focus on her new discovery. The shirt had to be the same shirt she had seen in Marlo's house. It was the same fabric, the same color and design, with the elaborately mono-grammed initials. But what on earth could Marlo have seen in Alex? Trying to think of him objective-ly, she had to admit that he could be considered handsome. Marlo did know him, yet, not in the same way Tish did. She probably didn't know he was a bully and had always been one, even as a child. She hadn't gone to school with him. Perhaps if she, Tish Jamison, didn't work with him, didn't know what he was like as a kid, perhaps she would think of him differently. It still seemed doubtful, but, really, it was not her place to judge what Marlo saw in Alex. She simply had to accept the facts as they presented themselves. As Tish drove, she was aware of a parade of recalled images darting through her mind. She saw how Alex and Marlo looked at each other on those occasions when Marlo visited the office. She remembered Mary had often phoned looking for Alex when he was supposed to be working. And Marlo had confessed to being involved with a married man. Tears began to trickle down Tish's cheeks. She had thought she was finished with tears for Marlo. The tears now were full of anger. How could beautiful, talented Marlo throw away any of herself on such a degrading, illicit affair with a shallow, worthless person like Alex! Tish remembered Marlo's decision about whether or not to tell Joseph, now Tish understood. Poor, poor Marlo.

Tish drove to her father's house. She found him in his study talking with a client. She paced, anxious to share her information with him. The grandfather clock in the hall chimed the hour in hoarse, bass tones. It was the only clock in the world, she assumed, that had grown hoarse from years of ticking. Sinking into one of the large cushioned chairs in the room adjoining the study, she drifted into a half sleep, jumping every now and then. It was the kind of sleep her mother referred to as noodle-nodding. When she heard the study door open and the departing remarks of the client; she was on her feet instantly.

"Daddy, it was Alex!" she said rushing into the study.

"Who?" Charles Jamison looked at his daughter, not grasping what she meant.

"The man Marlo was seeing!"

"How do you know?"

Tish explained her reasons for naming Alex.

Her father looked intently at Tish, "Does he know that you suspect him?"

"No," Tish reassured him, beginning to see the fear in his eyes.

"Tish, if he was the one involved with Marlo, he is probably the one who killed her. You may be in danger. I want you to stay in this house, do you hear?" He was talking to her as if she were twelve years old again.

"But, Daddy, I have things to do . . . he doesn't know I suspect. Look how many weeks it's been. If he were going to come after me, wouldn't he have already?"

"Not necessarily. He probably felt pretty safe when Emmett was in jail and the whole town was convinced they had the right man. Even if he considered putting you out of the way, he might have been waiting for a good opportunity. He probably hesitated because another murder would take some of the heat off Emmett. Now that Emmett's out, he could kill again and have everyone think Emmett has struck again."

Mr. Jamison paused, then said, "Tish, it all depends on his basic nature. If he killed in temper, or as we say, committed a crime of passion, he may be incapable of premeditating a murder. On the other hand, if he is tormented by the fear of you discovering his guilt, he may feel driven to kill you."

"Daddy, can't you just go to the sheriff and tell

him? Can't they arrest Alex?"

Her father shook his head sadly, "Tish, we have no real proof. The evidence against Emmett is still stronger than what we suspect about Alex. The fact that you saw his shirt in Marlo's house is all that we have to tie him to the case. Even if we could prove a relationship between them, which is doubtful, we have no proof that Alex murdered Marlo. Alex is a pillar of the community, carefully erected by our society's haphazard system of values. He is active in the church, a member of the Board of Trustees of a church college. Tish, he is one of those people who can lie and be believed. Emmett, on the other hand, is merely the soil of the community. He could tell the truth all day and not be believed. People don't want to find that their social outcasts have more integrity than their chosen preferred. That would force them to admit making an error of judgment."

"But, Daddy, the jury would be composed of all kinds of people. Surely some of them would see the truth." Tish clung to her idealism, to grasp for hope.

"Yes, thank God for our jury system. It's the only reason I've been able to live with my profession." His eyes looked fondly at the long row of law books which lined the shelves in his study. "And, Tish, we don't have evidence to convince the District Attorney. He would never put a man of such social position on trial without evidence that was conclusive."

Tish nodded, understanding.

"I wish we could do something, I'm really worried about Emmett," her father shook his head sadly.

"He's safe."

"You know where he is?" he asked.

Tish knew it would be useless to lie, "Yes, but don't ask me where."

Her father nodded. He sat quietly for a moment before telling Tish to take care. "We will find a way, God willing, to set things right. Try to be patient."

Tish left, promising to come back to spend the night. She didn't know what to tell her mother. She wouldn't be able to tell her about Alex for fear that worry would give the whole thing away.

Emmett woke to find his water jug empty. His head felt like it was on fire. Touching the crudely sutured wound, he knew it was oozing blood. Raising himself unsteadily from the cot, he staggered toward the stairway. Pausing to rest, he heard movement in the kitchen above him. It was so dark in the cellar there was no way of knowing if it was night or day. Cautiously, he moved toward the outside entrance and peeked through the crack in the door. It looked as though dusk was approaching . He would make his way back to the cot until the house was asleep. He hoped it would be soon, his tongue felt parched and swollen. It was strange that he couldn't remember drinking all of the water. Fitfully, he dozed trying to forget the thirst. Sometime later, fever raging through his body, he felt a hand gently shaking his shoulder. He opened his eyes to see a luminous face. The face looked something like him. He wondered if it could be a relative he didn't know. When he reached an arm to the stranger, there was no one there. Emmett tried to shake the fever from his head.

"This way," the figure beckoned from the stairway.

Emmett followed the figure to the stairs. By the time he reached the first step, he felt himself sinking. The figure was again beside him, helping him up the stairs. The mysterious man helped him into a chair at the kitchen table, then poured him a glass of ice water. Emmett gulped it down gratefully. Again the glass was filled. Emmett saw that there was food on the table just as Tish said there would be, but he had no appetite. A bowl of fruit was placed before him by the quick hand of his helper. Emmett felt compelled to eat it. When he had finished, he started to move the bowl from the table.

"No need for that," was the stranger's comment.

"Are you sure?" asked Emmett, still unable to grasp the situation.

"Sleep," the man admonished, leading him again to the stairs.

Emmett made his way back to the cot and quickly fell asleep. He dreamed, slipping in and out of consciousness. Awake again, he felt an arm behind his head. Someone was holding the water jug to his lips. This time it was full of cold water. He hadn't remembered to take it to the kitchen with him, but someone had. It was the stranger, of course, he thought, and opened his eyes to watch the man sponge his face with cool water.

Tish quickly swallowed the breakfast her mother had placed before her. Rebecca Jamison was completely bewildered by her daughter, as usual. She was glad that Tish had come to spend the night, but she couldn't understand her request for a sick call to her office when she was obviously not ill. It was unlike Tish to play hooky from her job. Rebecca also wondered why Charles was behaving so complacently about their daughter's behavior.

Tish grabbed her jacket and darted for the door hoping to avoid any explanation.

"Tish, where are you going?" her mother was not to be outdone.

"I've got to see somebody, I'll be back later." She left, determined to avoid any further questions.

Tish was greeted warmly at the Freeman home. She knew she would have to bide her time until she could find an opportunity to go to the cellar. She was worried about having to leave Emmett alone for so long. Tish listened as the sisters chattered away in their sing-song voices. She watched Rupert groom his feathers to a glowing ebony sheen.

"Papa ate more last night than he ever has since

he's been on the other side," Miss Dora was saying brightly.

"Really," Tish tried to sound casual, her heart racing.

"Yes," Miss Dora went on, "he had company, too. I heard them talking. It was another man, but I didn't recognize his voice. I don't know if it was someone from this side or that side."

Tish was dumb-founded. She was having difficulty maintaining her composure. "What do you mean?" she asked, "the other side . . . "

"Of death, child," Miss Dora explained politely.

"Oh . . . " Tish forced a nod. "Miss Dora, could I please borrow one of your pickling crocks?"

"Why certainly. Just stop by the cellar on your way out and take whatever you need. What are you going to pickle this time of year?"

"Uh, uh . . . some relish." Tish had no idea what was in season. All she could think of was getting to the cellar to see if Emmett was still there. If the sisters heard two voices, it must mean that Emmett had been discovered. Impatiently, she waited until both sisters were occupied so they wouldn't be tempted to accompany her to the cellar. Quickly, she said her goodbye and made her way out. Gently pushing open the door to avoid crashing against the cans, she entered and found Emmett asleep on his cot.

"Emmett, wake up," she whispered.

Emmett opened his eyes and studied the face

bent over him. "Miss Tish, it's you this time."

"What do you mean, this time? Who was here before?"

"I don't know." Emmett felt his head, "Someone helped me last night. I was sick with fever."

"Oh, you were probably delirious." Tish was relieved. "How are you feeling now?"

"Much better, in fact, I think all the fever has gone." Emmett then related how the mysterious man had helped him.

"Listen, Emmett, either you were out of your head or there really is a ghost in this house." Tish shivered at the thought, remembering that Miss Dora said she heard two voices. "Here, let me have a look at my needle work." Tish bent over to study the wound more closely. "I'm not sure how it's supposed to look."

Emmett grinned, "I feel much better and the throbbing is gone so it must be healin' good."

"Emmett, I hate leaving you here alone, but I'd better go. Try to be patient. Daddy is still working on your case. We have an idea who may have killed Marlo."

"Don't worry none about me, Miss Tish. This here is a whole lot better than bein' in jail."

After leaving Emmett, Tish decided the best way to relieve her tension was to take a ride on Ginger. The rain of the day before had been followed by the season's first frost. Tish was glad for the cold. Ginger would be full of vigor and would demand her full attention. Maybe she would be able to forget about Marlo, Alex and poor Emmett for a little while. The frost had caused the ground to form a field of tiny blades of ice in the barn lot. Tish enjoyed the feel of them crunching beneath her boots as she walked to the barn. Tacking up Ginger hurriedly, she mounted and charged off in a dash neglecting the customary warm up. Without really thinking, she found herself headed in the direction of the old Jones farm. No, it was no longer the Jones farm, it was the Darrin place, she corrected herself. Ginger was enjoying the crisp air as she moved briskly along the familiar trail. Neil was turning his tractor at the end of the field when he saw the horse and rider. He smiled. Tish was covered with a long scarf wrapped high about her face and a toboggan pulled snugly over her ears. Although he couldn't see any of her features clearly, he would have recognized her even if she had been on a different horse. No one else sat a horse exactly like Tish, he observed. He pulled the tractor closer to the fence row, and waved her to a halt. Tish was reluctant to admit to herself that this was what she had hoped for. It had seemed unlikely that she would run into Neil, but luck was with her.

"Why are you in such a hurry?" Neil called down to her.

"Just for the fun of it," she laughed.

"Want to help me spread manure?"

"No, not really," Tish said with a smile.

Neil looked at his watch, "Have you had lunch?"

"No."

"Well, you can have lunch with me then."

Tish looked at Ginger and frowned. "I don't know what to do with her." The little mare was in such good condition that she was not breathing hard, but was apparently ready for a rest.

"We'll put Ginger in the barn while we go inside." He climbed down and walked over to horse and rider. Swinging up behind her, he put one arm around her waist feeling how small it was. From his seat on Ginger's rump, he pointed Tish towards a newly renovated barn.

Neil put Ginger into a little paddock which adjoined an open shed. "She can stretch her legs or loaf inside. I like to give my horses a choice." Neil said, then turned to guide Tish through the back door of the house and into the kitchen. It was the first time Tish had been in the old house in years. It was bare except for essential pieces of furniture. She could not help noticing that it wasn't very tidy either. Neil watched Tish and smiled as he saw her wrinkle her nose in disapproval.

"I haven't had time to do anything with the house yet," he explained. "I guess I'll try to fix it up this winter after I get the pastures and hay fields as ready as I can this year. I've been spreading lime. This ground really needs it; it's been fallow so long, the sage grass has about taken over."

Tish nodded.

Neil pulled a big pot from the refrigerator. "I made chili last night. Hope you don't mind leftovers." He put the giant pot on the stove and returned to the refrigerator for a pitcher of ice tea.

"Looks like you made enough for a week!" Tish laughed.

"I did. It saves me time to make a lot of whatever I'm making."

While Tish set the table, she was thinking how she would fix the house if it were hers. She could see some old-fashioned white curtains on the windows, leather and rough tweedy fabrics on the furniture in the den which was located just outside the kitchen, some good paintings of horses and farm scenes on the walls. Her old mule-yoke mirror would look nice hanging by the coat rack.

"What are you studying?" Neil asked.

Tish blushed at her own thoughts. "Oh . . . just how good the chili smells." What business was it of hers to think of redoing his house, she thought.

They enjoyed the hot chili. Afterward, they went to sit by the fireplace.

"Tish," Neil said, "I have been wanting to see you. I've just been so rushed with work since the Mountain Ride, I really haven't had time. Do you think you could enjoy spending some time with me like this, keeping me company while I work, letting me visit you when I can? Later, when I get caught up, I'd like to take you places."

"What places?" Tish smiled.

"You know, places a guy normally takes his date . . . restaurants, movies, wherever you want to go."

"Places are really not all that important," Tish said, "not nearly as important as the company you keep."

Neil got up. Reaching for Tish's hands, he pulled her up. "I'm really glad you feel that way. It's just that you are a very special girl and special people deserve more than leftover chili."

They both laughed and went out into the cold. Tish knew her parents would be worried since she had been gone for a long time. She went to saddle Ginger and Neil walked back across the field to his tractor. As they bid each other goodbye, both knew they would be seeing each other again.

Although she needed to get home and relieve her parents' anxiety, Tish let Ginger walk slowly so she could savor the time she had just spent with Neil. She chided herself for experiencing pleasure while Emmett was hidden away in a cellar. Yet, she could not diminish the special elation she felt. Even the landscape appeared brighter, she noticed, bathed in the cool hue of the waning sun. There remained a crispness in the air but she was warmed by the vibrant golden leaves and russet meadow grasses.

"What a beautiful day, Ginger! Don't you agree?"

CHAPTER FOURTEEN

Alex noticed that his conscience had been easier to deal with than he feared. After the initial shock of his crime had subsided, he had been able to convince himself that it was only an accident that Marlo died. He had almost convinced himself that the fall to the floor killed her, not his hands around her throat. What he feared most, he admitted to himself, was being found out. Now that Emmett Moss was thought to be guilty, Alex had begun to feel his old sense of security. Secretly, he was glad Emmett had escaped. He was glad, not because of Emmett's innocence, but because his escape had further convinced everyone in Jensen's Valley of his guilt. His affair with Marlo would remain a secret, soon to be forgotten even by himself. He watched as his secretary placed the day's mail on his finely polished desk. Thumbing through it, he noticed a letter from the state office. The letter contained a memo which read:

"In response to your telephone message yesterday stating that there would be a delay in your quarterly report, you are instructed to have the report in our office no later than November 2. Failure to do so will result in suspension of funds to your district."

"Geez, that's my salary!" Alex blurted out.

"What?" Mabel peered at him over her jeweled glasses.

"It's due tomorrow! The mail must have been delayed getting here. Surely, they meant to give us more time than that! We'll have to type it up today and I'll have to deliver it all the way to Nashville tomorrow."

"If you have it ready, I'll type it right away," Mabel said brightly.

Alex gave her a threatening glare, "It's not ready. Damn that Tish." He would have to write it himself. Maybe Jenny could do it, but she was out in the field, probably wouldn't be back for hours. He pulled some copies of old reports from the files. Complimenting himself for his cleverness, he decided to rewrite an old report. Smugly, he sat down and began writing. The day passed more quickly than he would have desired. At last, Alex was satisfied with his product. He looked up at his secretary. "Mabel, you'll have to come back tonight to type this. I'm going to run it out to Tish's right after dinner and get her to proof it. Surely she can do that even if she is sick. Can you come back about seven?

"Certainly, sir," Mabel said calmly. She really wanted to tell him to try typing it himself. She had made plans for the evening, but she needed to keep her job.

Charles and Rebecca Jamison were relieved to see their daughter.

"I was afraid you were lying in a ditch somewhere!" Rebecca said, giving vent to her worry. "Your father kept telling me the horse would have come home by itself if you had taken a spill, but I wasn't so sure. Ginger seems to love you so, I wasn't sure she'd leave you."

After the evening meal, Tish announced that she was going to her cottage for a change of clothing.but was coming back. Tish entered the cottage leaving the door ajar. She was thumbing through the closet looking for her green blouse when she heard a car in the driveway. As she walked from the bedroom, she saw Alex walk through the open door. She did not notice the sheaf of papers under his arm. Alex had never come to her place before. She could not help wondering if he had come to harm her.

Alex was about to explain why he had come when he noticed the fear on Tish's face. Then, he knew she must suspect him. Why else would she be so afraid.

"What's the matter, Tish?" he asked knowingly,

"Nothing, Alex. You just startled me, that's all." Tish fought for composure.

Alex wanted to believe her. Yet, how could he be certain. He had to find out what she knew. "Tish, did Marlo tell you anything before she was killed?"

"Why, no." In spite of herself, Tish began to tremble.

"Oh, come off it, Tish, I can tell by the way you're acting, you know all about it, don't you!" Alex stepped forward. "It's written all over your face."

Tish turned to run, but Alex caught her by the back of her blouse. The fabric tore, but not enough to free her from his grasp. Alex grabbed her arms and turned her to face him. "How did you find out? Did you tell anyone?"

"I don't know what you're talking about," Tish tried to sound convincing.

"It doesn't matter now what you say!" Rage had begun to distort Alex's features. "Killing you won't bother me half as much as killing Marlo. I loved the bitch, but she was going to dump me for that fancy politician, just throw me away like I was nothing. Don't you see, I couldn't let her go to him. But you . . . you're such a know-it-all. You'd like nothing better than to ruin me. I'm not going to let you!"

Tish saw hatred in the violent eyes that were glaring at her. That was the last thing she saw before his fist crashed against her sending her reeling to the floor. Again, she felt a blow, she wasn't sure where it struck her. Her entire body was throbbing.

The room began to spin. Then it was dark. Somewhere deep in her consciousness, she wondered if Emmett would spend the rest of his life in the cellar at the Freeman place. She wondered who would take care of Ginger. Then she saw the faces of her parents, of Neil, Julie and Marlo. She wondered if she was on the other side.

Alex continued to plummet her body with brutal blows. He didn't hear the voices yelling at him. "Stop!" Charles and Neil Darron charged into the room. Alex was knocked unconscious when Neil struck him with the butt of the gun he was carrying. The two men hovered over Tish in helpless fury.

"She's alive, I feel her pulse!" Neil said in relief.

"Thank God," the father's words were barely audible, he reached over to touch her bruised face, with silent tears, grateful prayers.

Neil phoned for an ambulance and the sheriff while pointing the gun at Alex in case he came to. The sheriff and the ambulance arrived at about the same time. As paramedics loaded Tish onto a gurney, Sheriff Tompkins looked at Alex in shocked disbelief until Tish's father told him that he and Neil had both heard Alex confess to Marlo's murder. Alex had regained consciousness. He refused to say anything and simply glared at everyone including the sheriff while being read his rights.

Later, in the hospita,l friends and relatives of the Jamison family kept a constant vigil. Julie and Jimmy came and waited. Julie seemed to be in a state of shock. How could such a thing happen to her two best friends. Marlo was dead, and Tish seemed to be barely alive. She and Jimmy decided they would forget having a big wedding and would just go to the courthouse and get someone to marry them before anything else happened. Although the murderer was behind bars, Julie did not want to be alone. When Jimmy said he had to go to work, she begged him to stay. Hours passed, then another day and another night. Tish remained unconscious. The doctor tried to calm those who waited.

Slowly, Tish began to see the darkness diminish. The sea of faces around her began to come into focus. "Where am I?" she asked as she began to look around the room.

"You're in the hospital," her mother spoke softly, letting grateful tears stream down her cheeks. Gradually, her mother explained the sequence of events that had taken place since the beating..

"You have broken ribs, a concussion, and you look like hell," her father volunteered. "You're all black and blue with a bit of purple here and there."

Tish started to laugh until the pain in her ribs stopped her.

"Now, if we can only find Emmett," her father said, "this whole thing could be put to rest."

"Oh, poor Emmett!" Tish tried to sit up. "He's in the Freeman cellar!"

Everyone laughed. Charles Jamison left hurriedly to go to Emmett. Her mother stepped out of the room allowing Neil some time alone with Tish.

"Why were you with Daddy when he came to rescue me?" she asked.

"Well, you told me you were staying with your parents for awhile. After you left me, I couldn't get you off my mind so I decided I'd quit early and take a chance on seeing you. I planned to take you out into the cold night, figured I'd have a good excuse to keep you close to me." He held her small hand in his calloused palm. "And, Tish, that's what I wanted . . . you, close to me."

"On my way to your folks, I saw a car going to your cottage. When I mentioned that to your father he jumped up and asked me to go with him. That's when we found you."

Every muscle and bone in Tish's body seemed to shout its pain, yet she could not remember feeling so good inside. She felt Neil's lips on her forehead just before she began to drift into a peaceful sleep.

In her dream, she could see Emmett and Mattie and their children busy up on the mountain. She saw the rushing white water of Crazy Creek and heard the happy bluegrass sounds of Emmett and his band. And she felt Neil's hand on hers.

ABOUT THE AUTHOR

Sarah Simpson Bivens is an award-winning journalist for work published in several Tennessee media markets: the *Tri-County Observer* and regional *Southline Magazine*, Madisonville, the *News-Herald*, Lenoir City, where she once served as community life editor and reporter. She and her husband, Ron Bivens were co-editors and publishers of the *Loudon County Independent*, Loudon.

A native and resident of the area, she lives on a farm with her husband, three horses, two dogs, and eight cats where she enjoys trail riding and painting.

Crazy Creek is her debut novel

41215908R00126

Made in the USA
Lexington, KY
05 May 2015